"8 Mandates for Social Media Marketing Success *will help every marketer understand that 'catching fish' on social media isn't just about being in the right place. It's also about having the right tools and techniques. The 154 innovative marketing practitioners, authors, and professors featured in this book provide useful tips and techniques for 'reeling in' success for each mandate.*"

Dr. William J. Ward
Social Media Professor at Syracuse University

"*A truly unique take on social media mastery. This book is full of ____ ys from some of the best minds in ____*

Mark Schaefer
Author of *Return On Influence: The Revolution* ____ *of Klout, Social Scoring, and Influence Marketing*

"*Kent is a leader with respect to guiding the C___ in the social marketing space. He is a magnet for all of us who have banded together, taking a leadership role and stepping up to change the way marketers and brands build relationships and emotional connections with consumers. I consider his book a must-read for all business leaders.*"

Ted Rubin
Chief Social Marketing Officer at Collective Bias

"In a book that prizes listening above all else, Kent Huffman makes sure to take his own advice by letting others do the talking for him. This book is absolutely filled with countless bits of practical advice, poignant anecdotes, and real-life success stories. By keeping the information simple and accessible, Kent provides a brilliant model for aspiring B2B marketers trying to figure out how to put theory into practice."

Cheryl Burgess
Co-Founder, Managing Partner, and Chief
Marketing Officer at Blue Focus Marketing

"8 Mandates for Social Media Marketing Success *is a truly social book. Kent Huffman reached out to the people in his famous lists of top marketers on Twitter for their thoughts and stories to define the eight key factors of SMM success. This novel approach was probably natural for the co-founder of* Social Media Marketing Magazine *and mentor to marketing people on Twitter. It proves to be a very effective way to get these ideas across and motivate action. How appropriate that Kent wrote the first 'social' SMM book!* 8 Mandates *belongs in the hands or on the iPad or Kindle of anyone involved in marketing."*

Dr. Gary Schirr
Marketing Professor at Radford University

"8 Mandates for Social Media Marketing Success *is a revolutionary collection of case studies and social media success stories from every sector of business, both B2B and B2C. It is rare to find such a comprehensive assemblage of social media marketing guidance from such knowledgeable and diverse sources. Kent has excelled in providing an all-inclusive guide for today's leaders and marketers in any industry."*

Amy Howell
Founder & CEO of Howell Marketing Strategies

"Kent Huffman found a void in the market and filled it masterfully. A careful curator of content, Kent documents best practices in social media marketing and captures actionable insights from some of the sharpest minds in social media.
8 Mandates for Social Media Marketing Success *provides inspiration and plenty of customizable blueprints. Read it and tweet!"*

Teri Lucie Thompson
Chief Marketing Officer at Purdue University
and author of *Tuning into Mom: Understanding America's Most Powerful Consumer*

"8 Mandates for Social Media Marketing Success *takes ethereal propositions like 'listening' and places these into a practitioner's context, with a problem-solution-results format that will be familiar to any marketer. In combining case studies with the viewpoints of some of the most recognized thinkers in social media, Kent and Company have left us all with a practical desk-side reference—no small feat in a digital age."*

Frank Strong
Director of Public Relations at Vocus | PRWeb

"The expansion of the Internet has irrevocably changed the way marketers reach out to customers and consumers, now and in the future. This radical transformation of the marketing landscape, replete with mega opportunities and pitfalls galore, is the subject of Kent Huffman's brilliant new book, 8 Mandates for Social Media Marketing Success. *The book combines leading-edge insights from those who've 'been there and done that'—including marketing pros, professors, and authors—with pertinent case studies and examples of successful social marketing campaigns that met their goals and objectives through innovation, inspiration, and a bottom-line, biz-focused approach. Lots to learn, highly recommended!"*

Deborah Weinstein
President of Strategic Objectives

"Concise and backed by real-life expertise! Kent's ideas, covered in this book, will inspire you to re-examine your social media marketing perceptions and initiatives. His eight mandates framework provides a complete social media marketing business picture, with key insights and examples provided by practitioners that are suitable for both small and large organizations."

Alan See
Chief Marketing Officer at MindLeaders

"I count Kent Huffman as a colleague, a client, a friend, and now an amazing author for whom my respect has further swelled. Kent's book is meaty and goes down easy with golden bullets of social media genius ready for you to discover."

Eve Mayer Orsburn
Founder & CEO of Social Media Delivered
and author of *The Social Media Business Equation: Using Online Connections to Grow Your Bottom Line*

"Numerous renowned practitioners, authors, and teachers of marketing, branding, and design from around the world have contributed their insights to 8 Mandates for Social Media Marketing Success. *I have no doubt this book will be a huge success!"*

Beto Lima
Marketing Professor at Faculdades Integradas Hélio Alonso

"Kent Huffman's book should be taking up permanent residence on the desks of everyone working in social media marketing, as well as business owners looking to close the gap between their brands and their customers. The easy-to-digest format—compelling commentary from top names in marketing and academia, along with success stories from companies large and small—makes 8 Mandates *a handy guide for navigating the social media marketing waters."*

Renay San Miguel
Chief Content Officer at Splash Media and former anchor/reporter at CNN, HLN, and CNBC

*"*8 Mandates for Social Media Marketing Success *condenses the thoughts and credence of leading practitioners in social media and, in turn, provides an undiluted guide to essential best practices of effective social media. Building community is one such practice that is built upon time and trust. This book demonstrates how, with clever curation and through the power of engagement, you can commence your journey into building a trusted core community of fans and followers."*

Dr. Dean Anthony Gratton
Co-author of *Zero to 100,000: Social Media Tips and Tricks for Small Businesses*

"This book is a must-read for any organization preparing to put a toe in the social media waters. I particularly appreciate Kent's chapter on listening. Far too many organizations dive into the deep end without first tuning into the conversations taking place online, and you can find their abandoned social outposts littered across the Internet. I'd also emphasize the chapter on leadership. Being successful with social media requires leaders to take thoughtful risks . . . it requires character and courage, and Kent is someone who leads by example."

Sima Dahl
President of Parlay Communications

"I used to judge the Echo Awards for the Direct Marketing Association, and I learned so much reading the case studies and results. So imagine my delight when I opened Kent Huffman's book and discovered that more than 150 social media pros have contributed their 'takes' and success stories in a great, concise format: organization, challenge, solutions, results. Whatever your program, you'll pick up some great ideas here. I did!"

Lois K. Geller
President of Lois Geller Marketing Group

"Not only do the eight mandates make a lot of sense, they're all supported by commentary from countless experts from around the world. The insights presented in 8 Mandates for Social Media Marketing Success are bolstered by short, tight case studies from a wide range of organizations. The book is a quick read with a focus on how businesses achieved results."

Chuck Martin
Author of *The Third Screen: Marketing to Your Customers in a World Gone Global*

"Social media has forever altered the way brands communicate with their stakeholders. For your brand to stand out, grow, and succeed in this ever-changing social world, you need an objective social media marketing strategy and tools that transform approaches and ideas into actions and results. What's most enriching about this book is that you'll find not only Kent's strategies and tools but insights from marketing pros from around the world and case studies from a variety of leading B2C and B2B companies. 8 Mandates for Social Media Marketing Success *should be on the bookcase of every marketing executive.*"

Berenice Ring
Marketing Professor at Fundação Getúlio Vargas

"The challenges and opportunities for businesses in this digital age are enormous. Today's B2B marketer must understand how to leverage social media marketing to drive revenue and ROI. Kent Huffman's book provides successful strategies that define the 'what' and 'how.' This is a must-read for any brand looking to build a successful social marketing campaign without hitting any stumbling blocks along the way."

Mark Burgess
Co-founder of Blue Focus Marketing and Visiting
Marketing Professor at Rider University

"Imagine a high-energy dinner party with smart friends freely sharing lessons learned from years of practice, research, and reflection. A party where the host purposefully builds the guest list and guides the conversation. That's 8 Mandates for Social Media Marketing Success. With this book, Kent Huffman curates insight on social media marketing from leading CMOs, authors, and professors. The no-nonsense introductions ground us in the context of social media as a marketing discipline, and the case studies bring the wisdom to life. The book's elegant organizational construct makes it fast and engaging. 8 Mandates is a delight."

Margaret Molloy
Partner & Chief Marketing Officer at Velocidi

"Kent has created a masterful resource for social media marketing. He has done the nearly impossible—distilling social media guidance into its most essential mandates. Unlike most books on this subject, Kent's eight mandates will remain relevant regardless of what new social media platforms may be created in the future."

Alicia Arenas
Founder & CEO of Sanera Professional Development Company

"In 8 Mandates for Social Media Marketing Success, Kent Huffman expertly illustrates the joy, wonder, opportunities, and challenges of the social media platform. This book is a practical and informative must-read for businesses and their leaders engaged in reputation building using the social media channel."

Lida Citroen
Principal of LIDA360 and author of *Reputation 360: Creating Power through Personal Branding*

"8 Mandates for Social Media Marketing Success is a groundbreaking book. Kent Huffman has built a strong framework for social media marketing and backs it up with real world case studies and validation from more than 150 CMOs and marketing practitioners."

Chris Herbert
Chief Marketing Officer at Mi6 and co-founder of Silicon Halton

8 Mandates for Social Media Marketing Success

Insights and Success Stories from 154 of the World's Most Innovative Marketing Practitioners, Authors, and Professors

By

Kent Huffman

Published by C-Suite Press
P.O. Box 341360
Austin, TX 78734 USA

**8 Mandates for Social
Media Marketing Success**

Insights and Success Stories from 154 of the World's Most Innovative Marketing Practitioners, Authors, and Professors

www.8Mandates.com

ISBN 978-0-615-68164-1
Published in the United States of America

Dedication

8 Mandates for Social Media Marketing Success is dedicated to my parents, Dr. Louie C. Huffman and Dorothy M. Huffman. Both were successful educators. My father was a college mathematics professor and administrator for 35 years, and my mother taught several subjects at the grade school level for 33 years. Although they obviously didn't teach me the mandates for social media marketing success, they did a great job of educating my two sisters and me about the mandates for living a productive, successful, and meaningful life. I thank, honor, and love them for that.

This book is also dedicated to Wounded Warrior Project, which is featured on page 110. This highly respected organization raises awareness and enlists the public's aid for the needs of injured service members, helps them aid and assist each other, and provides unique, direct programs and services to meet their needs. I am proud to do what I can to assist the caring people who are involved with Wounded Warrior Project and hope you will join me in supporting their efforts.

Table of Contents

Author's Note

About a year ago, I made the decision to write a book about social media marketing—one that fills in some of the blanks. In the following pages, I've focused on the personal behavioral traits that can affect your marketing initiatives, and this book details what I consider to be the top eight social media marketing mandates that must be mastered in order to, simply put, get results.

What makes this book different, and also infinitely credible, is the manner in which the content has been gathered. Some of the most innovative marketing practitioners, authors, and professors—154 of them from around the world—have provided their take on the eight mandates in this book. You can be sure that every comment by every one of those professionals comes with a big dose of "been there, done that" and "we know what works."

One other approach that makes this book unique is the manner in which the success stories have been researched, written, and organized. At the end of each chapter are two B2C and two B2B success stories featuring "big fish" (large organizations) and "little fish" (small/medium organizations).

Speaking of fish, shortly after completing the first draft of this book, I rewarded myself by going bass fishing at my weekend getaway on Lake Fork in East Texas—a favorite pastime that I don't get to pursue as much as I would like. I suppose I can blame my CMO responsibilities at BearCom Wireless and Co-Publisher duties at *Social Media Marketing Magazine* as having something to do with that.

Nevertheless, I found myself fishing off my boat dock early that Saturday morning in really unforgiving Texas summer heat—not the best of conditions. After a couple of hours, the only bites I had gotten were nibbles, which told me that the fish in the immediate area were so small they couldn't get their mouths around the lure (or that I was just rusty).

At first, I didn't pay a whole lot of attention to Sammy, whose name I would learn later. As he and his boat grew closer to my dock, I became intrigued by how Sammy moved about on the water in "stealth mode," using a foot control connected to the trolling motor on the bow of his boat. I noticed he had several fishing rods laid out behind him, with what appeared to be a different lure attached to each one. The guy sure looked prepared, I'd give him that!

I watched Sammy's effortless cast—a flick of the wrist that placed his lure just where he wanted it almost every time. He really knew how to make his line dance. But playing the part is one thing; actually catching something is another.

As Sammy moved closer to the dock, I decided it was time to leave. He could have that empty hole I'd been fishing. With my rod in one hand and tackle box in the other, I was just stepping off the dock when I heard Sammy's voice. "Gotcha!" I stopped and looked back over my shoulder to see his rod tip jiggling as he quickly reeled in a nice bluegill sunfish.

Cast after cast brought in more bluegills. At this point, Sammy had my full attention, even though the little voice in the back of my mind was saying, "What a piece of luck."

When Sammy finally reeled in an empty line, he had moved close enough to the dock that I heard him mutter to himself, "So that's how it's gonna be, eh? The big guy runs off the little guys." Curious, I watched as Sammy switched to another rod with a different lure.

Moments after the next cast, the rod tip dove straight downward, almost touching the water's surface. This was no bluegill, that's for sure! Sammy jerked his rod with just the right tension to set the hook and began reeling. After the fish passed under the boat a couple of times, Sammy brought it to the surface, and wow! This was a nice largemouth bass, at least four or five pounds!

That little voice in my head was no longer mouthing off about luck. This guy knew what he was doing. No sooner had the bass been placed in the boat's livewell than I watched Sammy's lure hit the water again. This time, the rod tip actually did touch the water when it bent down, as the strike was fierce.

Sammy knew he had hooked something special. Carefully, he used his foot-controlled trolling motor to move his rig out to deeper water, while at the same time masterfully reeling and pulling. As his catch went deeper under the boat, I could hear him say, "Oh, so you wanna play, huh?"

Finally, Sammy was able to wrangle the fish out from under the boat. He then let his prey run in a series of lateral movements, slowly pulling it closer. After what seemed an eternity, the fish broke the surface, and I gasped. This was no four or five-pounder. It was what bass fishermen call a "hawg!"

I watched, enthralled, as Sammy landed the hawg, removed the hook from its gaping mouth, and held the massive fish up to the sky. He then turned and looked at me, grinned broadly, and said, "And on my 50th birthday!"

Within a few seconds, Sammy had the monster bass on his scales. Almost nine pounds! He turned and asked if I would take a picture with his cell phone, and I was more than happy to oblige.

After Sammy and I parted ways, I couldn't help but think that fishing and social media marketing have a lot in common. Sammy was experienced. He was disciplined. He was certainly patient. He was prepared. He knew what bait to use. He had the right gear—tools if you may. And he obviously knew where the fish were. Those are some of the same traits that a good marketer needs to succeed in the social media world.

The mandates in this book—used consistently with discipline and patience—will, without question, elevate your social media marketing skills. And as a result, you'll catch a lot more fish . . . oops, make that customers.

Kent Huffman
Kent Huffman is an accomplished marketing and customer experience executive. He currently serves as the Chief Marketing Officer at BearCom Wireless and is the founder and Co-Publisher of *Social Media Marketing Magazine*, a new digital publication written by the leading CMOs, marketing book authors, and marketing professors around the world who are active on social media. Previously, Kent held the positions of Vice President of Marketing at CompuCom Systems, Global Marketing Communications Director at Perot Systems (now Dell Services), and founder of his own boutique marketing consulting firm, Marketek Media. Kent has a bachelor's degree in marketing from Texas State University and is accredited as a Certified Business Communicator (CBC) by the Business Marketing Association. Kent is the co-founder of the CX|M Institute and sits on the Customer Experience Corporate Advisory Board for the CMO Council.

Foreword

By Dr. William J. Ward

I first "met" Kent Huffman several years ago on Twitter through his work with *Social Media Marketing Magazine* and his "Top Twitter" lists: Top CMOs on Twitter, Top Marketing Book Authors on Twitter, and Top Marketing Professors on Twitter. I soon began to notice that almost every time I discovered something new and useful about social media marketing, Kent was already there and had developed relationships with many of the experts.

Kent has a passion for learning and sharing the newest and most effective tools that can help us understand and improve social media marketing. When he and I finally met face to face, I was pleased to discover that in addition to social media marketing, we also share a passion for fishing. And since you've already been introduced to the *8 Mandates for Social Media Marketing Success* by Kent through a fishing reference in the Author's Note, it seemed only appropriate to begin the Foreword with a nod to fishing.

I grew up on a small lake in Rockford, Michigan, where my dad taught me how to dig for worms for bait and find the "honey hole" on any lake. Both my parents encouraged my entrepreneurial spirit, and at the age of nine, I had a thriving bait business, selling worms and sharing fishing tips with my customers. Ever since, I've followed the philosophy to "keep digging for worms;" i.e., continue learning from the best and sharing with the rest. Kent's fishing metaphor in his Author's Note and the insights and success stories shared throughout this book reinforce the value of learning from the best and sharing what you learn with others.

8 Mandates for Social Media Marketing Success will help every marketer understand that "catching fish" on social media isn't just about being in the right place—it's also about having the right tools and techniques. The 154 innovative marketing practitioners, authors, and professors featured in this book provide useful tips and techniques for reeling in success for each mandate.

I've never seen a fisherman talk a fish onto the line or into the boat, so the first and last mandates on "listening" are my favorites. The lessons learned from repeatedly listening well and then acting upon these lessons create a continuous cycle for adding sustainable value. Social media enables so many new opportunities for listening that it is a crucial mandate for social media success.

An old Chinese proverb teaches that to give a man a fish is to feed him for a day, but to teach him how to fish is to feed him for a lifetime. Kent Huffman and the *8 Mandates for Social Media Marketing Success* ensure you won't go hungry anytime soon.

Keep digging for worms!

William J. Ward

Dr. William J. Ward

Dr. William J. Ward, a.k.a. "Dr4Ward," is the Professor of Social Media with the S.I. Newhouse School of Public Communications at Syracuse University. Bill is an American Marketing Association Hugh G. Wales Outstanding Faculty Advisor of the Year. He has often been quoted by the media, including the *Wall Street Journal*, *USA Today*, the *New York Times*, the *Huffington Post*, *NPR*, and the *Associated Press*. A frequent speaker on the topic of social media, Bill has been featured at Harvard University, SXSW Interactive, various American Marketing Association chapter events, and the Environmental Protection Agency. He also teaches internationally and is involved with the Cannes Lions International Festival of Creativity. Bill earned his Ph.D. in media and information studies at Michigan State University. When he isn't fishing, Bill enjoys connecting students with professionals to help them learn about all forms of communication and creativity.

Introduction

Navigating the Maze

The social media landscape consists of many communication channels. That in itself creates layers of complexity. Add the behavioral traits that marketers must learn and apply in order to effectively engage with their customers, employees, and other constituents, and, quite frankly, everything can start to get a bit murky. It's a lot like getting lost in a maze. Which turn do you take next?

Successfully navigating the social media maze requires a clear understanding of how social media works. But it's not enough to just know how to use all the channels and tools. That's the easy part. A close examination of how other marketers have been successful with social media reveals that it requires a more strategic approach.

The Mandates

The eight mandates detailed in this book focus on the behavioral traits of the leading social media marketers and how they incorporate listening, planning, relationships, trust, leadership, community, and value into their social campaigns. Putting all the mandates into practice in a thoughtful, cohesive way—using the strategies and best practices outlined herein—will undoubtedly lead you to success.

Expertly Generated Content

What makes this book different is the unique manner in which our information has been gathered. 154 marketing practitioners, authors, and professors were interviewed for their perspectives on what it takes to launch and maintain effective social media marketing campaigns. These interviews present a wealth of ideas and wisdom on the eight behavioral traits that every social media marketer must master.

Just How Big Is Social Media?

Jake Hird, Senior Research Analyst at London-based Econsultancy, has this to say about the scale and scope of social media:

"The sharing and dissemination of information is the metaphorical currency of the digital environment, and in this sense, it's important to recognize that, theoretically, the entirety of the web is social. As the Internet continues to race toward becoming an everyday expectancy in the life of every individual across the planet, the importance of the social web cannot be underestimated—culturally, politically, and commercially.

However, the noticeable shift in what has largely been a philosophical concept of a truly connecting, virtual space is rapidly becoming a reality. In the past, information was created and curated by a few, but through the evolution of social media, the currency of the realm has been given to the many.

Inarguably, the technologies, platforms, tools and modes of individual production, ownership, and sharing of information—collectively referred to as social media—have been the catalysts for this shift. This is enabling the development of the social web to happen at a pace never seen before now.

A well-cited example: It took 38 years for radio to reach 50 million listeners and 13 years for terrestrial TV to capture 50 million viewers. And it took four years for the Internet to reach 50 million people. But in less than nine months, Facebook added more than 100 million users.

What learnings can be taken from this? Inherently, we all are social animals, and the technological enabling to find our own social groups—wherever they may be on earth—is quite literally on steroids. The speed and growth of uptake amongst the social web is quite unbelievable, and the size of the platforms used is near incomprehensible. And yet, we are only at the tip of the iceberg.

Consider that the ideology of the Internet is to connect all individuals around the globe; however, only one third of the world is currently a part of this. But factoring in the undeniable fact that technology is rapidly becoming cheaper and more available—along with the forming infrastructure to support a truly social web—it's clearly apparent to see the direction in which this is heading overall.

From a marketer's perspective, there is potentially enormous commercial value in social media—just as there has always been profit where the masses are. Given the sheer size and activity across the social landscape, those who choose to ignore it, do so at their own risk.

Social media provides not only a platform for users to connect online but also a platform for marketers to connect with users. With billions of people using social media literally every minute of the day, the only real question that remains is whether your marketing efforts are a part of their interactions."

Social Media's Global Reach

With the advent of social media, global commerce is now at your fingertips. The fact is, the moment any organization, individual, or mom-and-pop business puts up a LinkedIn page or publishes a blog post, it has "gone global," whether that was the intent or not.

Global social media marketing, however, comes with a new set of challenges. Whether it's a giant corporation like AT&T or a small business like Cellar365.com, the messages you send, what you promote, and how you promote can vary by country, region, and locale. Knowing a country's language and its culture is the first step toward connecting. In the case of a channel like Facebook, an organization may need multiple pages, each one constructed to target the nuances of a specific market.

In addition, marketers must pay attention to the channels that are available in each marketplace. In Germany, for example, it's not Facebook, it's studiVZ. And it's not LinkedIn, it's the very popular XING. In Brazil, South Korea, China, and the Netherlands, a variety of other country-specific channels have been adopted.

In other words, the global impact of your social media marketing efforts will be determined not only by adhering to the mandates in this book but also by fully understanding how to best approach an audience in any given geo-market.

Increased Mobility

Mobility is the next big shift for social media marketing. Communication is rapidly moving away from the desktop to smartphones and tablets. No longer are you tethered to your office. In the car, on a bus, at the airport, or even at home, marketers can reach out and touch their customers and other constituents 24x7x365, thanks to the availability of a wide variety of new mobile devices.

Mandate #1:

Start Listening

By now, you've probably noticed that listening is both the first and last of the eight mandates for social media marketing success that I've highlighted in this book. That's because I believe it's the single most important key for marketers who want to be successful in social media.

Although the average person spends about 45% of his or her waking hours listening, most of us are simply not very good at it. Various studies conducted over the years have shown that we comprehend and retain only about 25% of what we hear!

With that challenge so prevalent, applying good listening strategies and skills in the social media environment becomes even more critical. "Intentional listening," as my friend and colleague Eric Fletcher calls it, should be front and center in your social media marketing strategy, as it plays an integral role in ensuring that you can find your target audience, hear and understand their wants and needs, and then effectively communicate with them in such a way that establishes trust and strong, long-lasting relationships.

At the outset of your social media marketing program—even before implementing your listening tactics—do your homework. Conduct surveys and focus groups. Gather responses and evaluate. And spend some quality time "lurking and learning" on Twitter, Facebook, LinkedIn, and other social media channels to find out what your target audience has to say.

Finally, make sure you're carefully monitoring your competitors as well. Are they listening to their constituents or just broadcasting marketing messages? You'll have to do a little old-fashioned detective work, but remember that with social media, the playing field truly has been leveled. You don't have to guess about who's doing what—just listen.

WHAT INNOVATIVE CHIEF MARKETING OFFICERS HAVE TO SAY ABOUT THE MANDATE TO "START LISTENING"

"My marketing philosophy is grounded in the A, B, Cs (About the Customer, Build the Brand, Combine Art and Science). 'About the Customer' means listening, as there is simply no substitute for carefully listening to the customer. And nowhere is that more important than in social media. We attain more 'likes' and 'shares' on Facebook and more retweets on Twitter when we ask questions of our fan base or respond to their questions. Rather than talk at our followers, we build a conversation with them. Through constant monitoring of what is being said, we can engage with fans and followers to address their questions or concerns. Then we're rewarded with messages, photos, and posts that further increase engagement. It becomes a virtuous cycle of sharing and problem solving that builds the brand."

Teri Lucie Thompson
Chief Marketing Officer at Purdue University

"Social media has shifted the listening paradigm for our brand. It allows our team members to conduct personal member communication with more immediacy. Secondly, it allows us to discover opportunities and issues that may have never bubbled up to management. Finally, our aggressive pursuit and monitoring of the social media conversation leaves our members with the knowledge that we care and want to provide a great fitness experience."

Tony Wells
Chief Marketing Officer at ADT Security Services

"Effective marketing is about relevance. I was tired of mass marketing when I got my third round of Groupon offers for flying trapeze lessons and eyelash enhancement. Through social media, we can listen and respond accordingly."

Jeff Hasen
Chief Marketing Officer at Hipcricket

"As a brand marketer, consider focusing more on the 'social' and less on the 'media' when it comes to social media. Brand advocates share because they are passionate about something and feel connected. The best connections come from relationships, and relationships are ideally cultivated with listening first and talking later—not the other way around. Let's not forget, all things being equal, people prefer to buy from people they like."

David Alston
Chief Marketing Officer at Radian6

"The voices are out there.' Yes, that could be a movie title or part of a dialogue in a horror story. But the truth is that to achieve a higher level of creative strategy, you must find ways to stay connected with what's being said all the time. The most successful projects I produced were inspired by what I heard or read on digital media. I remember when the company first came with a caution alert about using social media; I was already the number one user of LinkedIn, Facebook, and Orkut. Nowadays, I am a heavy user of Twitter, and digital media is mandatory. I learned how important is to listen to the (digital) voices out there. It is a way to stay connected and ageless."

Marcello Coltro
Chief Marketing Officer at MGM Networks Latin America

"Your brand is the sum of the conversations that are happening about you—in real time. Your brand is no longer what YOU say it is or what your advertising says it is, it's what's your CUSTOMERS are saying about you. Marketers must become effective listeners, so they can effectively participate in the discussion. Context and relevancy are now the cornerstones of effective marketing. We're no longer in an era of 'one size fits all' marketing messages."

Tim Kopp
Chief Marketing Officer at ExactTarget

WHAT INNOVATIVE MARKETING BOOK AUTHORS HAVE TO SAY ABOUT THE MANDATE TO "START LISTENING"

"Mom was right—you have two ears and one mouth, and listening is the number one communication skill in all walks of life. Once you put aside the desire to push your message and start listening, you'll know what to do next. Treat people with the kindness you show to those close to you. Follow your company rules and procedures, but remember there is a human being talking to you. Listen and love. It's as simple as that."

Warren Whitlock
Co-Author of *Twitter Revolution: How Social Media and Mobile Marketing is Changing the Way We Do Business and Market Online*

"Engagement—or more basically, having a conversation—is an essential part of making an impact with social media. In any exchange between people, you need to really pay attention to what is being said, so you can be fully and authentically engaged. That means you need to listen to what's on their minds, so you understand what matters to them. If you don't, you're not going to have meaningful, relevant, touching, or useful conversations that resonate with the audience. The result is that your information won't be shared, and worse yet, it will be ignored. And you'll miss the ideas and opportunities that arise from people connecting with one another."

Robbin Block
Author of *Social Persuasion: Making Sense of Social Media for Small Business*

"Brands can utilize social media as a vehicle for insights, ideas, and customer engagement, but the dialogue needs to start with listening to stakeholders. Listening is not about leaving all decisions about the brands to external stakeholders—strong brands are confident about what they want. But a good dialogue starts with an exchange of initial views—this is where social media can make a difference to global brands in the future."

Martin Roll
Author of *Asian Brand Strategy: How Asia Builds Strong Brands*

"The reality is that people are talking about your company, whether you choose to acknowledge it or not. Today, every facet of your organization—good and bad—manifests first in social media. Social media listening is the ultimate canary in the coal mine—it's the early warning detection system for the modern age. Some companies are reluctant to get involved in social listening, because what they hear isn't always positive. But social listening is always a NET positive. Whether it's customer service, business intelligence, real-time marketing, or a combination of them all, eavesdropping on your customers and prospects is an opportunity that every business should seize."

Jay Baer
Author of *The Now Revolution: Seven Steps to Becoming
a Faster, Smarter, and More Responsive Company*

"A brand is a promise delivered, and listening and responding are the most critical components to delivering that promise. Whether you like it or not, there are people everywhere talking about your company, making their opinions public online. Social media gives consumers a revolutionary voice. Therefore, every company should have a CLO—Chief Listening Officer. They are the air traffic controller of the online communication for your business. CLOs watch, listen, and direct all customer feedback to the appropriate departments or people within your organization. And the goal of a CLO is to capture what consumers are saying about you and engage with them, ultimately adding value by extending customer service and converting enthusiastic consumers into brand ambassadors and evangelists."

Jeffrey Hayzlett
Author of *Running the Gauntlet: Essential Business
Lessons to Lead, Drive Change, and Grow Profits*

WHAT INNOVATIVE MARKETING PROFESSORS HAVE TO SAY ABOUT THE MANDATE TO "START LISTENING"

"Listening is the secret to social media marketing success. It seems the best conversationalists are always the best listeners, and social media is all about the art of conversation. Listen for the good, the bad, the ugly. Find out not only what people are saying about your brand and its products or services, but also about your competition and industry. Keep in mind that you can't delegate effective listening to monitoring tools, though they should be part of your toolkit. Transforming followers into brand advocates comes with active listening and sharing based on the needs and interests of your community. Active listening that extends beyond 9-5 is the best way to gather the business intelligence you need to effectively promote your brand, build a community, avert a crisis, and leapfrog your competition."

Glen Gilmore
Forbes Top 10 Social Media Power Influencer
and Adjunct Professor at Rutgers University

"Social media presents a unique opportunity to have conversations and interact directly with consumers. Businesses must remember that active listening is paramount. Neglecting to listen attentively can result in a missed opportunity to understand your customers or offering customers dialogue with no substance."

Jessica Rogers
Adjunct Professor at Texas A&M University and Southern New Hampshire University

"Listening—it's the critical key to being successful in using social media! Imagine social media as creating a horizontal flow of information, with producers creating messages and audiences receiving and then commenting on that information. I envision social media as a way of moving groups—any type of group—from apathy to action. It's only by listening to our target audiences that we can create messages of value and build trust-based relationships because people know they're being heard."

Dr. Nancy Van Leuven
Professor at Bridgewater State University

"The success of my work on social networks can be attributed to the creation of relevant marketing content for my target audience—after carefully listening to that audience. It can also be attributed to the implementation of a policy of permanent support for people who are initiated into the 'Web 2.0' world and who share quality content. In other words, I first select my target audience: What do they need? What do they want? Who are they? I then evaluate the content to be shared with them—depending on the pertinence, relevance, and allure for this target group—in order to maintain high levels of interaction."

Andrés Silva Arancibia
Professor at the Universidad Andrés Bello

"Actively listening on social media will enable you to collect vital customer information that is important to different areas of your organization, such as innovation and customer service."

Dr. Christine Moorman
Senior Professor at Duke University

"A key characteristic to building unbreakable relationships is investing in the relationship and knowing what is important to the other person. In order to know what is necessary to build a particular relationship, you have to simply pay attention. 'Relationship architecture' at it's core is putting the focus on other people and understanding their needs, likes, dislikes, and anything that makes up the fabric of what they are all about. The only way to do this is to stop talking and start listening. I realize that you have probably heard that advice before, but listening doesn't just mean hearing. If you are not digesting the hints and tidbits the person is revealing about herself, you are missing the point and opportunity. You must pay attention and truly listen if you do not want to squander the potential of a relationship."

Lou Imbriano
Professor at Boston College

Gatorade

The Organization

Owned by PepsiCo, Gatorade is a leading sports performance and fuel innovator, as well one of the world's largest sports brands.

The Challenge

Gatorade was in the process of transforming the brand from a leader in hydration to a leader in sports fuel. Social media was identified as a significant opportunity during this transformation, as it allowed for observation and interaction among a substantial number of athletes on a daily basis. Social media also created the opportunity for Gatorade to get a clear view into athletes' perception and understanding of the Gatorade brand and the linkage of sports fuel and sports performance.

The Solution

At its Chicago headquarters, Gatorade established Mission Control, a digital command center that leverages social media activity to garner real-time consumer insights to drive business action and strengthen Gatorade as a leader in the conversation. Mission Control is staffed by members of Gatorade's PR, digital, and media agencies, who each provide specific expertise and responsibilities. Seven data visualization screens help the team track relevant and real-time brand, competitive, athletic, and nutrition topics. By listening and engaging with consumers via social media, the brand is using Mission Control learnings to reinforce Gatorade as a sports performance and nutrition leader.

The Results

Since the launch of Mission Control, Gatorade has seen a significant increase in the volume of conversations around the brand and sports nutrition, adding to its credibility as an innovator. Now, 70% of Gatorade mentions are relevant to sports performance, sports fuel, and core brand equity topics, allowing Gatorade to better understand the target consumer, support new product development, and inform media spending.

Submitted by Sarah Bild, Senior Manager of Digital at Gatorade

Restaurant.com

The Organization

Restaurant.com serves as a "community matchmaker" by introducing great restaurants to great people. The company helps restaurateurs promote the new and unique aspects of their eateries while providing diners with great value in a fun, new, and cost-effective way.

The Challenge

When Restaurant.com launched more than ten years ago, it was one of the first daily deal sites—before the term "daily deal" was common nomenclature. With the growth of social media and Restaurant.com's increasing presence on social channels, customers were presented with a new outlet of inquiry that had to be closely monitored and addressed. Even though Restaurant.com was a veteran in the daily deal space, there was still a hurdle to jump with brand awareness and trust for potential and new customers who were just joining the Restaurant.com family. Strong phone and e-mail support was always a staple of the Restaurant.com business, but the company needed to do more to retain its position as a leader in social customer care.

The Solution

A new full-time team was formed to intently listen across all social media channels and to monitor, respond in a timely fashion (within two hours), and provide exceptional customer service 24x7. The urgency with which issues are now handled by the new team is strong evidence of the high value that Restaurant.com places on listening to help enhance the customer experience.

The Results

Since the inception of its social media listening program, Restaurant.com has fielded more than 5,000 questions on Facebook and Twitter, averaging 300 to 500 per month and closer to 900 during peak season. The program has also led to higher customer satisfaction levels, repeat purchasing habits, and additional word-of-mouth recommendations.

Submitted by Lauren Sleeper, Director of Social Media Strategy at Likeable Media

Motorola Solutions

The Organization

Motorola Solutions is a leading provider of mission-critical communication products, solutions, and services for enterprise and government customers. Through leading-edge innovation and communication technology, Motorola Solutions is a global leader that enables its customers to be their best in the moments that matter.

The Challenge

When President Obama signed into law the Middle Class Tax Relief and Job Creation Act of 2012 (HR 3630), he reserved the 700 MHz D Block spectrum for public safety. This legislation would spark changes throughout the public safety communications industry, and Motorola Solutions needed to educate its customers on its impact and opportunities. Traditional "blanket the sky" marketing tactics would be costly and might swing wide; this required a new approach that was extremely targeted and relevant for the right audience.

The Solution

To better target key influencers, users, and those interested in D Block, Motorola Solutions launched a social media listening campaign, tracking keywords using Visible Technologies as the primary platform and Design Kitchen as the agency to interpret some of the data. The tool was able to specify the volume of conversations and where those conversations were taking place—including websites and social media channels—as well as sentiment.

The Results

Insights provided by the listening program allowed Motorola Solutions to target the right online publications and the right audience, build relationships with nine key influencers, and start relevant conversations with more than 150 people seeking information and education about the D Block legislation. Motorola Solutions will use the data to build an editorial calendar of blog posts based on topics suggested by users and constituents.

Submitted by Cherilyn Stringer, Senior MarCom Consultant and Jennifer Mesenbrink,
Global Editor-in-Chief of Integrated MarCom at Motorola Solutions

Faegre & Benson

The Organization

Established in Minneapolis in 1886, Faegre & Benson is a B2B law firm that serves clients throughout the United States, Europe, and Asia. It has been recognized by independent third parties for excellence in client service, technology, culture, and corporate citizenship.

The Challenge

Faegre & Benson believes that deep industry expertise and a vaunted track record helps the firm to attract new clients and that quality service and attention to detail enables it to retain them. To that end, the firm has always looked for new ways to stay on top of what's going on in its clients' businesses. But that meant that Faegre & Benson was constantly faced with trying to keep up with reams of information in the marketplace so it could brief its clients and respond in a proactive manner. So the firm launched a search for a technology tool that would make that process more effective and efficient.

The Solution

After a thorough search and evaluation process, Faegre & Benson selected Manzama, a business and social intelligence platform that allows its legal users to stay updated on client, practice, and industry developments, while also keeping abreast of competitive intelligence. The online service listens to the market by searching and analyzing industry-specific news sources, blogs, Twitter feeds, and a variety of other social media channels.

The Results

Where Faegre & Benson's marketing and business development staff once needed to track down important and relevant information proactively, that data now finds them. Manzama uncovers and categorizes the information that really matters, so Faegre & Benson's legal professionals can better manage, market, protect, and grow its practice. In addition to generating an average of 8-10 leads per month, this tool also enabled individuals to reduce market intelligence research hours by 75% on average.

Submitted by Peter Ozolin, CEO & Chairman of Manzama

Mandate #2:

Plan Carefully

Too many marketers jump right in and start using various social media tools and technologies—such as Twitter, Google+, and blogs—before they've even developed a strategic plan or thought about how those activities might impact the rest of their marketing initiatives. Don't make that mistake! Take a little time to determine how to best integrate social media into your existing marketing strategy and mix. It'll pay off for you.

Step one in the planning process is to nail down specific social media objectives, based on the listening activities detailed in Mandate #1. Now that you know what your constituents care about and are discussing on social media, how does that impact the messages you need to communicate to them? Step two is to integrate your social media strategy into your overall marketing strategy to ensure your resources can be leveraged most efficiently and effectively and that common goals can be more easily reached.

If you work for a large enterprise, you have two significant advantages over a small business when it comes to planning and budgeting for a social media marketing program. First, your company's DNA most likely has a built-in "think strategically" strand, and second, it also probably has a fairly large wallet. If, however, you work for or own a small business, you have an advantage as well. You most likely can make strategic decisions and launch new marketing programs fairly quickly. That can be a huge benefit in the fast-paced social media world.

Finally, be sure you're prepared to monitor and measure your impact and progress. Establishing benchmarks and other metrics that can be tracked over time will help you better understand what's working and what's not, and thus be able to make whatever adjustments are necessary to ensure the success of your social media marketing activities.

WHAT INNOVATIVE CHIEF MARKETING OFFICERS HAVE TO SAY ABOUT THE MANDATE TO "PLAN CAREFULLY"

"Social media is not to be trifled with. It's as important to your brand as any TV commercial or magazine ad. Customers expect that when they want to interact with your brand in social media, you will be responding. Therefore, throwing up a Facebook page or Twitter account that occasionally gets monitored is not sufficient. You have to plan. Planning for how to deal with the conversation that is social media is as important as being there in the first place. Who is going to interact with customers? How often will the sites be monitored? What will you do if your customers become negative? You will need answers to all these questions and more if you are going to be a socially smart brand."

Lisa Gavales
Chief Marketing Officer at Express

"Rookie marketers rush headlong into the fray. Set goals for social media first, then create your plan to achieve them."

Christopher Krohn
Chief Marketing Officer at Restaurant.com

"'Adventure is just bad planning.' So said Roland Amundsen, the leader of the first Antarctic expedition in 1910. Bad planning for him could have had deadly results. Luckily, the stakes aren't so high for those of us managing social media, although it often feels a little too adventuresome for comfort. But it needn't. Yes, social media is inherently unpredictable. And no, you can't control it. But you can and should plan for all contingencies. Planning begins by understanding why you engage in social media in the first place and what you hope to achieve. Planning assures that your organization is prepared to truly engage and deliver on the social part of social media. Planning considers the potential outcomes— both good and bad—of opening up this two-way channel with your stakeholders."

Brian Kenny
Chief Marketing Officer at Harvard Business School

"Shiny objects reflect light and attract the human eye by giving the impression of motion. Similarly, social media can create a mirage of value and visibility, but it can also fall short unless it is based in a well-constructed plan designed to achieve your business objectives. The basics are more important than ever—understand your audience and what is relevant to them, focus on your overall and channel-specific objectives, determine your strategic approach, and then deploy the technologies and tactics that will deliver the results you are seeking. Avoid the social media shiny object trap by planning and bringing direction to your activities."

Dwight Griesman
Chief Marketing Officer at Forrester Research

"The big fascination with online marketing of the 1990s was based on a completely new level of measurability. Since then, online marketers have been trained to set goals, build integrated programs, constantly measure success, and optimize for best results. Yet, strangely, a lot of marketers jumped into social media as if the rules of online marketing did not apply, when in fact, social media has only exponentially escalated and accelerated the level of interactivity known from e-mail, search engine optimization, banners, and other 'Web 1.0' programs. In social media, your message can be scrutinized, praised, loved, or hated in front of audiences that snowball from one to hundreds and thousands in a matter of hours, sometimes minutes. This new marketing means of unprecedented power certainly calls for the same—if not much tighter and more disciplined, yet agile—planning and execution."

Britta Meyer
Chief Marketing Officer at Socialtext

WHAT INNOVATIVE MARKETING BOOK AUTHORS HAVE TO SAY ABOUT THE MANDATE TO "PLAN CAREFULLY"

"Planning is at the heart of a successful social media initiative. Aimlessly posting Facebook updates and sending out tweets will not result in valuable business outcomes. Planning helps you develop measurable objectives and build a strategy for listening, creating content, engaging with stakeholders, and measuring program effectiveness. Skip the planning, and you may as well skip the program."

Deirdre Breakenridge
Author of *Cyberbranding: Brand Building in the Digital Economy*

"Too many social media marketing efforts are developed in a haphazard or even arbitrary way. They are rushed, poorly planned, or based on imprecise thinking. Instead, take the time to plan carefully. For social marketing to be effective, the strategy, content, social media platforms, and timing must all work in concert to achieve specific goals and objectives—measurement and monitoring are also keys. After all, marketing is a means to an end, not an end in itself. Furthermore, remember that social media turns conventional marketing on its head. Success is dependent on building relationships by sharing great content and creating fantastic experiences, rather than bombarding your target audience with your message. By providing exceptional value, you'll help passionate customers spread the word—you'll be 'all the buzz.'"

Frank Sonnenberg
Author of *Marketing to Win: Strategies for Building Competitive Advantage in Service Industries*

"Without a plan, there is chaos. A profile on every social media platform isn't a plan. A plan starts with understanding your audience and developing content that suits both them and the platform they spend the majority of their time on. You can and should plan your social media success."

Simon Salt
Author of *Social Location Marketing: Outshining Your Competitors on Foursquare, Gowalla, Yelp, and Other Location-Sharing Sites*

"So often, business people use social media with no plan. That's fine as long as you won't later expect that some 'thing' was accomplished. But if you seek or will be held accountable for results, a plan is requisite. There's much buzz about monitoring and measuring social media activity, but most easy-to-obtain volume and reach metrics are rather useless without defining objectives and establishing baseline measurements at the planning and goal-setting stages. Just because you can measure something doesn't mean you should; context matters. Reaching masses of 'the wrong people' isn't very valuable. Lack of context is precisely why we see so many frustrated executives when marketing types present general follower metrics. Solid planning describes whom you seek to interact with, as well as a successful level and type of interaction."

Michelle Golden
Author of *Social Media Strategies for Professionals and Their Firms: The Guide to Establishing Credibility and Accelerating Relationships*

"Planning carefully is critical to the success of any social media marketing campaign. You need to first start with a strategy or conversion goal, and then look at the social media tools that will best achieve that goal. Too often, companies start with a tool—say Facebook—and then try to fit a strategy into Facebook. It needs to be the other way around. An example would be a conversion strategy that states, 'increase your Twitter followers,' then how you would use Facebook to drive Twitter followers; or a conversion strategy of 'build your e-mail list,' then how you can use your social media tools to accomplish that goal. Always begin with the conversion strategy, and then identify what tools will accomplish your specific goals."

Lon Safko
Co-Author of *The Social Media Bible: Tactics, Tools, and Strategies for Business Success*

WHAT INNOVATIVE MARKETING PROFESSORS HAVE TO SAY
ABOUT THE MANDATE TO "PLAN CAREFULLY"

"Careful planning with social media reminds me of preparing for a great road trip. Where do you plan on going? How do you plan to get there? What do you need for the journey? If you get a flat tire along the way, do you have the resources and training to fix the problem and get back on track? Planning allows for the unavoidable detours and encourages the freedom to explore new discoveries without fear of getting lost. Without a plan, it is easy to forget where you were headed. Careful planning is important because it helps keep you on the path to success and to measure your progress along the way."

Dr. William Ward
Professor at Syracuse University

"As marketers, we've been trained to plan. But it's a different type of planning that's required now. A social media marketing strategy should be a fluid and loose outline, rather than something that's rigid and detailed. It's something that needs to be reviewed—and probably modified—on a regular basis. Social media marketing is malleable and forever changing—and there's the whole 'human factor' that can make it very unpredictable. So build in some flexibility and include the option to change your plans, if necessary."

Kathy Magrino
Adjunct Professor at Rider University

"I always tell my students that when planning any type of marketing communication, the process itself is crucial. The plan will change as it is executed. That's the nature of operating in a dynamic environment. But it's the planning process—all the thought and effort that go into developing a strategically sound plan—that guides good decision making and ultimately determines success."

Dr. Joe Bob Hester
Associate Professor at the University of North Carolina

"Plan carefully, my friend. Plan your name or handle for social media—how will your brand be known (@yourbrand)? Plan the tone and personality for your communications—how will your brand sound? Plan the frequency of social media posts—how often will you communicate? Plan the type of content you will put out there—what will interest your audience? Plan how to get people to interact with you—what will move them? Plan how to respond if something goes wrong—a disaster plan is essential for social media. Plan to stick with it— once you start using social media, you can't stop without costs. And plan how you will celebrate your success—you deserve it!"

Derek Mehraban
Adjunct Professor at Michigan State University

"What is your organization's goal for your social media marketing campaign? This is an essential decision leaders should make before launching any initiatives in the digital space. An efficient social media marketing plan should be aligned with your brand's DNA, be customer-focused, and be strategically built as a lasting conversation. A rushed execution without careful planning may lead to no response—or worse—instant damage to your brand's reputation."

Berenice Ring
Professor at Fundação Getulio Vargas

"Planning properly can help in avoiding some critical missteps once a social marketing campaign has been implemented. A typical plan for a strategy will be inclusive of reviewing objectives, benchmarking current social assets and competitive assets, identifying opportunity gaps in conversations penetrated and conversations held, etc. In this fairly new medium, we sometimes cannot anticipate every single scenario, and a plan to quickly adapt should also be considered and incorporated."

Ruben Quinones
Adjunct Professor at New York University

Baylor Health Care System

The Organization

Founded as a Christian ministry of healing more than 100 years ago, Baylor Health Care System exists to serve all people through exemplary health care, education, research, and community service. Baylor has an extensive network of more than 50 locations throughout the Dallas/Fort Worth Metroplex in North Texas.

The Challenge

Women make nearly 80% of all health care decisions, so historically, Baylor's messaging had been primarily designed to speak to them. Facebook had recently become an enormously successful medium for Baylor, especially since health care is an industry in which emotion and personal stories are so ingrained in the experience. But Baylor wanted to also reach out to men. However, men are funny creatures—they need comfort and familiarity, as well as a bit of a challenge. So Baylor needed an innovative plan to break through to the male audience and make a significant impact.

The Solution

Baylor created an integrated marketing campaign entitled "It's a Guy Thing." The campaign centered around driving traffic to an online microsite that offered registrations for free men's health care events at several Baylor facilities. In addition to using more traditional marketing tactics—such as newspaper and magazine advertisements, TV commercials, direct mail, and opt-in e-mail—Baylor's marketing plan also included a mobile app, a QR code, and several social media vehicles: Facebook, Twitter, and YouTube.

The Results

Web-based registrations for Baylor's men's health care events soared by 215% after the campaign ran. Although direct mail and magazine advertising drove the largest number of registrations, Facebook was the primary contributor from the social media vehicles.

Submitted by Patty Reupke, Director of Consumer Relationship Marketing at Baylor Health Care System

Cellar365.com

The Organization

Founded in 1982, Eola Hills Winery in Rickreall, Oregon is a privately held company that began as a grape grower but transitioned into wine production, bottling a variety of table wines under its own label. The company sells 85% of its inventory in Oregon and Washington via the traditional multi-tier distribution system and through its tasting room.

The Challenge

Acutely aware that tasting room sales afford limited growth and that Eola had achieved limited success in other states utilizing a three-tier distribution system, the management team opted to expand sales activities by selling direct to the consumer. However, developing a plan that could be supported with the company's limited marketing dollars and in-house staff presented significant difficulty.

The Solution

Although the winery's existing website had a shopping cart for processing orders from its existing wine club members, reaching out to consumers in other states on a wide scale required a much more focused and creative approach. This became apparent upon evaluating the cost of a traditional promotional plan, which required the development of print collaterals, the purchase of mailing lists, and the placement of space ads in local and regional print publications. The answer: social media to reach the masses.

The Results

After a series of planning sessions, the company decided to build a companion website named Cellar365.com to promote "winery direct" sales and link it to the main site for processing transactions. The new site is keyword friendly and features a blog that discusses a variety of wine-related topics. To build interest, the winery tweets daily from @Cellar365 and has it own Facebook fan page. The end game is increased sales as a result of consumer demand. Production is expected to increase 40-50% over the next three to four years.

Submitted by Eric Rogers, Chief Financial Officer at Eola Hills Winery

IBM

The Organization

IBM is a global technology and innovation company offering a wide range of technology and consulting services. In addition to capabilities to enable collaboration and predictive analytics, a key strategic growth area for IBM is cloud computing, with the objective of helping companies and organizations accelerate business transformation.

The Challenge

Driving market awareness to increase consideration and preference for IBM is a key objective for cloud computing initiatives. The IBM marketing team required a strategy and tactical plan that elevated IBM's cloud computing experts among the online dialogue in this evolving and dynamic market segment.

The Solution

The cloud marketing team, after applying insights from social listening research and building up a robust collection of content, established an internal cloud community of subject matter experts. The community is managed by a dedicated social business leader who nurtures the conversation across relevant social venues. Fresh digital assets are shared weekly with community members for distribution. The strategy also incorporates blog content sourced from participants in IBM Redbooks residencies. In the residencies, IBM cloud technical experts learn about other cloud areas and receive training on participation in social media venues.

The Results

In the last six months of 2011, the cloud social venues realized 92% growth. Planning for 2012 includes continued focus on growing the program eminence through established social initiatives, including the program's monthly Twitter chat session, #cloudchat, which has already garnered more than 3.8 million impressions.

Submitted by Ian Gertler, IBM Social Business Enablement Leader (ITSO), Smarter Computing Social Business Manager, and Founder & Chief Marketing Officer at Symplegades

Freed Maxick CPAs

The Organization

Freed Maxick CPAs, P.C. is one of the largest accounting and consulting firms in Western New York. Serving closely held businesses, SEC companies, government agencies, and nonprofits across New York and around the world, Freed Maxick mobilizes its high-performance professionals to guide client growth, compliance, security, and innovation.

The Challenge

With formidable competition in the marketplace, an ongoing challenge had been the firm's inability to generate meaningful awareness and engagement in the Rochester community. The consequences of not having a strategic plan for community relations had also caused missed opportunities. How could the firm differentiate itself, be relevant, and "cut through the clutter," considering its limited presence? And what role could social media play?

The Solution

Freed Maxick implemented a detailed planning process to establish goals and innovative tactics for its social media marketing strategy. The firm designed and executed a digital Facebook billboard community campaign in Buffalo and Rochester, which displayed real-time content from its Facebook page. Freed Maxick also launched several other social media platforms to share content, including a Twitter newspaper, a LinkedIn site, a YouTube channel, a mobile website, and a recruiting website.

The Results

Freed Maxick's social media dialogue amongst new users grew by 400%, and Facebook fans more than doubled. The firm quickly became more recognizable with local nonprofits, building relationships with 30-plus new community groups. The firm also won several awards, including InfoTech Niagara's BETA award for social media, and it was named "Marketer of the Year" by the Rochester Chapter of the American Marketing Association.

Submitted by Emily Alexandria Burns, eMarketing Communications Specialist at Freed Maxick CPAs

Mandate #3:

Develop Relationships

A true relationship has to be earned. It's about respect and trust. And a balanced relationship is reciprocal. You do something for somebody else, and they do something for you. You exchange ideas. You use each other as a sounding board. For a relationship to last, it has to be a two-way street.

Followers on Twitter and friends on Facebook are not equivalent to relationships. Just as in the real world, a true relationship on social media has to go deeper than just a surface connection. Having 5,000 followers or 10,000 friends is meaningless if you don't truly connect. If you're not convinced of that, ask one of your Twitter followers for an opinion on that white paper you're writing. If nothing happens, you've got your answer.

One of the keys to nurturing real relationships on social media can be found in the manner of your engagement. People want to be valued, and once they feel you value them, they will most likely feel a connection with you—and some degree of loyalty—and will also continue to expect an ongoing dialogue to reinforce those feelings. And you'd better deliver if you expect the relationship to grow and strengthen over time.

Successful relationships are also about helping to support others. It's not all about you, your company, or your agenda. Social media is a community, and as a member of that community, you should not only contribute to it in various ways, but you should also recognize the contributions of others. For example, promoting other people's accomplishments by "liking" their videos, retweeting their tweets, or sharing their latest blog posts will go a long way toward building connections and real relationships. And don't let those relationships stop at the keyboard. Get to know your social media connections in the real world whenever possible.

WHAT INNOVATIVE CHIEF MARKETING OFFICERS HAVE TO SAY ABOUT THE MANDATE TO "DEVELOP RELATIONSHIPS"

"It is easy to fall into the 'more is more' trap when evaluating your social media friends and followers. But it is the downstream behavior that really matters. Do people return for more content or information? Do they recommend you to their own friends? Do they share their own ideas with you? I'd rather have 25 close friends than 1,000 casual acquaintances. Just like real life."

Seth Farbman
Chief Marketing Officer at Gap

"As a Turkish proverb states, 'No road is long with good company.' Social media is like an ongoing high school reunion, where relationships are constantly renewed and refreshed in order to remain relevant. Many of the connections with colleagues, customers, and vendors developed or augmented by social media become as important as those old high school friendships. What's different is that these relationships are productive—creating efficient ways to find and share insights, best practices, new business, and career opportunities."

Gail Nelson
Chief Marketing Officer at Siegel+Gale

"There are seven key steps to building strong relationships on social media. First, just be you—that approach is simple, honest, and sustainable. Second, go second— learn your friends' and followers' goals first. Third, give first—and don't keep score. Fourth, be valuable—become known for something and stay front of mind. Fifth, build trust—so you'll be invited to the 'real' party (I call this the back channel). Sixth, think equals—keep an eye on value and the social order, act like an equal, and don't jump too far or too soon, as collaboration is a game of approximate equals. And seventh, open doors—asking is essential, so ask early and often, but never ask too much, so you can leave the door open for the next round."

Nick Kellet
Chief Marketing Officer at List.ly

"Most marketers 'connect' through social channels, not just to learn about best practices and new ideas, but to truly engage with one another. In this case, 'engaging' is a two-way communication path where real people can have real conversations. By doing so, both parties feel more connected, and the social channel enables this authentic experience. A brand (as with an individual) must listen and engage with every possible individual that connects with that brand through social channels. If a brand does this, it will inspire its customers and create amazing brand advocates. Customers truly want a relationship (an emotional connection) with a brand. All the brand has to do is want it back—and embrace the power of social marketing."

Matt Corey
Chief Marketing Officer at Mass Relevance

"If you want to continue to reach your market in this social media age, the marketing focus needs to be on building relationships, and metrics need to expand beyond ROI (return on investment) to include ROR (return on relationship). Your consumers will recognize in a heartbeat if you are simply trying to get something from them—and they will not stick around. It's not that you aren't allowed to want anything from your consumers, it's that there must be a 'give' to go along with every 'take,' and that is what developing and maintaining relationships is all about. If you truly want to make an impact, aim to always put more energy and attention in your 'give' column than in your 'take' column. Relationships ARE the new currency—honor them, invest in them, and build emotional connections."

Ted Rubin
Chief Marketing Officer at Collective Bias

WHAT INNOVATIVE MARKETING BOOK AUTHORS HAVE TO SAY ABOUT THE MANDATE TO "DEVELOP RELATIONSHIPS"

"I grew up in a small town where everyone knew if you were a reliable, honest, and good person. The online world is even smaller. Be good to people and help them out, because you never know when the intern of today becomes the startup founder of tomorrow."

C.C. Chapman
Co-Author of *Content Rules: How to Create Killer Blogs, Podcasts, Videos, E-Books, Webinars (and More) that Engage Customers and Ignite Your Business*

"Developing relationships on social media is essential, since this is really about connecting people through the digital environment. Interestingly, relationships can more easily start in the digital environment, as like-minded people can be easily drawn to and aggregate around similar content and interests. And with the addition of mobile connectivity to the mix, more people—and relationships—can be developed while on the go."

Chuck Martin
Author of *The Third Screen: Marketing to Your Customers in a World Gone Mobile*

"I guess I'm old school. To me, 'social media' is just a new-fangled phrase; communicating socially has been around since the days before web browsers even existed. Back then, those of us communicating by Usenet, message boards, and e-mail discussion lists lived by a credo: Share, because we're here to help and support one another. If you abide by this, you can't help but develop relationships—many of which I still have today. Relationships forge trust, and openness to building trusting relationships translates into better business. These kinds of practices apply perfectly in today's social media world. Frankly, I prefer better—rather than more—social media relationships. In the long run, these few relationships serve me far more than thousands of so-called friends who really don't know me at all."

Hollis Thomases
Author of *Twitter Marketing: An Hour a Day*

"Marketing has always needed differentiation and memorability, but in traditional media, you didn't have to work to get it seen—you simply paid for eyeballs. But when the message needs to be shared to be seen, there's no direct link between dollars and media reach. Marketers face a major mind shift when approaching social media: you can't just buy attention. People are the media here. You need to nurture relationships with people over time to get your message to spread. Centering your effort on ideas that hold deep meaning for your audience creates an authentic connection and captures their support. Social media successes in marketing, politics, and social good result from honest, methodical relationship development."

Andy Smith
Co-Author of *The Dragonfly Effect: Quick, Effective, and Powerful Ways to Use Social Media to Drive Social Change*

"Social media is not a one night stand, but a lifelong relationship. Its value is found primarily in building relationships that lead to increased trust and customer loyalty. Its goal should be to turn strangers into friends, friends into customers, and customers into brand evangelists."

Paul Chaney
Author of *The Digital Handshake: Seven Proven Strategies to Grow Your Business Using Social Media*

"I think of a social media marketing program as a series of mini image ads. Nobody logs onto a social site to be marketed at. Boring! We want to learn things, say things, and interact with people—have relationships, in other words. Companies that can do this will be successful marketing in social media. It takes patience, but it works. And you have access to a world of people you might never meet in life!"

Lois Geller
Author of *Response: The Complete Guide to Profitable Direct Marketing*

WHAT INNOVATIVE MARKETING PROFESSORS HAVE TO SAY
ABOUT THE MANDATE TO "DEVELOP RELATIONSHIPS"

"What's new with social business is that customer engagement is not just a brand's connection with the customer. It is also the customers' engagement and relationships with one another in the horizontal, viral aspect. This is the true measure of success in real-time marketing and is what creates the long tail of engagement."

Beverly Macy
Professor at the University of California at Los Angeles

"In the world of social media, organizations and individuals need to understand that the most important word is not 'media,' but rather 'social.' For one of the first times in history, marketing communicators can truly 'communicate' with their current customers, potential customers, or constituents. Prior to social media becoming part of the marketing mix, most of marketing communication was not communication at all, but rather the one-directional pushing of messages out. By its very nature, communication should be bidirectional. Whether a relationship is personal or business-based, it is dependent on listening and responding as much as it is on speaking. While social media provides the tools and the opportunity, organizations must be prepared, willing, and open to communicating with their customers and constituents. The true value of social media will be realized by those who bravely take this step."

Lyle Wetsch
Associate Professor at the Memorial University of Newfoundland

"People have relationships with companies and brands, but before social media, those ties were usually casual and anonymous on the consumer side (sounds seedy, doesn't it?). With social media, those relationships can, and have, become one-to-one—providing marketers with real opportunities to interact, understand, and fulfill consumer needs."

Mike Johansson
Professor at Rochester Institute of Technology

"For brands, some say being human is the new black. Relationships are fueled by Twitter, Facebook, Google+, blogs, and other social enablers that help marketers engage in previously unimagined ways. Success in social media depends on making emotional connections across a multiplicity of touchpoints. In other words, success depends on making friends. In essence, a marketer must act like the prospector, sifting through a wealth of new connections until only the relationships of the highest value are left—the ones worth their weight in gold."

Mark Burgess
Visiting Professor at Rider University

"The key success factor in social media is regular engagement of targeted audiences for maintaining relationships over time. Relationships are the glue that binds your network together, with reciprocity being its catalyst. From passive information sharing to active problem resolution, genuine support evokes a responsive network that generates value for you in return."

Dr. Constantinos Coursaris
Associate Professor at Michigan State University

"There is no social media without social. There is no social without relationships. And there are no relationships without people. People are the basis of social media; however, the success of a social media strategy depends more on the relationships developed between people than on the individuals themselves. Therefore, developing and nurturing successful relationships is essential to being successful on social media—this is what social media is deeply about. I believe there are seven main pillars for supporting successful relationships: 1) ethics, 2) education, 3) values that drive the relationship, 4) selection of people to connect and interact with, 5) real interest in people, 6) availability to listen and interact, and 7) give first, receive later."

Martha Gabriel
Professor at HSM Educação

House of Fraser

The Organization

House of Fraser is a large British department store chain with 63 locations across the United Kingdom and Ireland. The successful national retailer was established in Glasgow, Scotland in 1849 as Arthur and Fraser and is well known for its high-quality premium brands offered at attractive prices.

The Challenge

One quality that has set House of Fraser apart from other department store groups in the U.K. is the commitment to building strong customer relationships by providing an imaginative, exciting, and relevant shopping experience. As its online presence grew, so did the desire to extend to the web this strong sense of engagement and belonging among customers.

The Solution

During the 2011 Christmas season, Bazaarvoice helped House of Fraser make major strides toward deepening relationships with its customers. Using Bazaarvoice's latest technology tools, House of Fraser launched a Christmas promotion entitled "You Shouldn't Have!" The promotion invited online visitors to share stories of the strangest, funniest, and most hideous Christmas gifts they ever received, with a winning entry ultimately chosen to get a Christmas stocking packed with House of Fraser brand goodies. To encourage participation, House of Fraser e-mailed customers who had written reviews or submitted questions on the website, or who had "liked" House of Fraser on Facebook.

The Results

The response far exceeded expectations. In just one month, 908 stories were submitted, surprising and delighting the House of Fraser management team. The e-mail and social media-fueled promotion also succeeded in reinforcing the idea of House of Fraser's website as an exciting, engaging shopping destination.

Submitted by Meghan Meehan, Brand and Communications Manager at Bazaarvoice

Lexus of Memphis

The Organization

As the certified Lexus dealer in Memphis, Tennessee, Lexus of Memphis provides new and used Lexus cars, parts, accessories, and service to drivers throughout the MidSouth.

The Challenge

While Lexus and its dealerships work very hard to maintain a reputation for luxury vehicles and being the finest dealer network in the industry, a communication barrier was identified in the Memphis area: the perception that Lexus is "too luxurious for me." Shoppers for vehicles, new or used, had too often avoided the Lexus of Memphis dealership for fear of impending "sticker shock" or because of a general negative connotation of car dealerships.

The Solution

With strategic guidance from Howell Marketing Strategies, social media accounts were established for Lexus of Memphis with the intention of strengthening relationships by communicating with its customers, potential customers, car enthusiasts, and residents of the MidSouth, no matter their vehicular affiliation. Facebook, Twitter, and YouTube channels were employed, and the Lexus of Memphis brand ensured that it was open and available on social channels and conversations were welcome.

The Results

By breaking down the communication barriers and becoming a personable brand through social media, Lexus of Memphis quickly generated positive results. Questions and answers, problem solving, referrals, and engagement with current and potential customers began to mount. More than 500 individuals who may never have visited the dealership in person became engaged with the brand. Inquiries about vehicular purchases and the sale of two cars in a two-month period were a direct result of activity on Twitter and exemplified the ROI from social media. And a relationship that began on Twitter has been developed with the corporate office at Lexus, leading to unique opportunities for the Memphis dealership.

Submitted by Kiersten Bagley, PR and Social Media Coordinator at Howell Marketing Strategies

AT&T

The Organization

With a powerful array of network resources that includes the nation's fastest mobile Internet network, AT&T is a leading provider of wireless, Wi-Fi, high-speed Internet, voice, and cloud-based services. The company also offers advanced TV services and one of the most innovative suites of IP-based business communications services in the world.

The Challenge

AT&T began noticing that business-to-business customers were turning to social media for product and service insights. Since AT&T wanted to have more one-on-one relationships specifically with its B2B audience, connecting with current and potential customers to share expertise, answer questions, and inform them about new products and services made perfect sense.

The Solution

As a way to build relationships with its B2B constituents, AT&T launched an internal ambassador program to get its employees out and interacting with customers on social media. A group of employees at AT&T soft-launched the Networking Exchange Blog to foster discussions with business leaders on technology innovations. Next, the company began promoting its blog and encouraging its participants to use their own Facebook, Twitter, and LinkedIn accounts to connect with B2B customers. Soon after, AT&T launched the Networking Leaders Academy, an educational program designed to improve the social media skills of its internal "experts."

The Results

In just a few months, traffic to the Networking Exchange Blog rose by 55%. Blog comments and social shares increased significantly as well. With the ultimate goal of shortening its B2B buying cycle, AT&T plans to further build out its Networking Leaders Academy program, providing a broader employee education base for social media.

Submitted by Cheryl Burgess, Co-Founder and Chief Marketing Officer at Blue Focus Marketing

MindLeaders

The Organization

MindLeaders changes lives through learning. The company's talent management and e-learning content solutions help both organizations and individuals meet the employee development, performance management, and managerial challenges of today's workforce.

The Challenge

Today's consumers connect and build relationships with their families, friends, business associates, and favorite brands on social sites such as Facebook, Twitter, LinkedIn, and Google+. That means brand pages on those social networks have become the new website, and social media must play an integral part in every strategic marketing plan. With goals of stimulating organic revenue growth, updating the company brand, and providing more relevant and targeted communications, the MindLeaders Board of Directors set customer relationship building through social media platforms as a top priority.

The Solution

An integrated and comprehensive social media marketing strategy and employee training program (with heavy focus on the sales force) was developed and implemented. In addition, corporate social media policies and procedures were documented and distributed. The initial social platforms that were addressed included Twitter and LinkedIn, while the tool sets utilized were TweetAdder and TweetDeck.

The Results

In the fourth quarter of 2011, the MindLeaders Twitter profile grew 300%. Retweets on Twitter increased 42%, and mentions grew 100%, showing improved engagement. The MindLeaders group on LinkedIn grew more than 50% as relationships expanded across platforms. As an added benefit, the MindLeaders Klout score increased 15%. Finally, inbound link growth to the MindLeaders website from major social platforms grew more than 400%. And most importantly, 2011 EBITDA increased 49% over 2010.

Submitted by Alan See, Chief Marketing Officer at MindLeaders

Mandate #4:

Establish Trust

The success of virtually every brand relies largely on the bond of trust generated between customer and company. That same bond can obviously be created between individuals as well. But as is the case with Mandate #3 (develop relationships), trust also has to be earned.

To begin with, authenticity is essential in your social media messaging. Whether you're speaking for your organization or yourself, always be you—just plain old honest you. Pretending to be someone you're not is a shortcut to a credibility gap, and that spells trouble in the trust-building business.

Being the real you—and growing the trust factor—needs to come with a good dose of personality as well. However, don't exhibit the steamroller mentality: a pushy, get out of the way, I'm on a mission-type attitude. On social media, it's too easy to distance yourself from people like that just by unfollowing or unfriending them. So instead, strive to be known as a thoughtful, considerate, supportive member of the social media community.

Exhibiting an inquisitive nature and a funny bone can help keep you in good standing, too. A great sense of humor is always an effective ice breaker and door opener.

In addition, strive to be as transparent as is reasonable. The more open and honest you're willing to be—and the more information you're willing to share—the more credible you'll appear. And always do what you say you're going to do. Nothing will impact trust in a positive way more than living up to your commitments.

As a marketer, you must realize that responsiveness also plays a major role in building trust. Especially when you're dealing with a complaint or other negative issue, be prepared to address it head-on, and do so quickly.

WHAT INNOVATIVE CHIEF MARKETING OFFICERS HAVE TO SAY
ABOUT THE MANDATE TO "ESTABLISH TRUST"

"With every new communication venue that becomes available to consumers, the imperative of trust becomes more pronounced. Not only does the believability of a brand drive followers, friends, and 'likes,' but—perhaps more importantly—it helps customers 'rise above' sometimes conflicting information that arises through these new consumer-driven channels."

Steve Fuller
Chief Marketing Officer at L.L.Bean

"Being real and authentic, as well as listening and engaging, are all elements of establishing trust in social media. Trust is important, as people who connect with you and your brand online are in a way endorsing you through association."

Ruth Brajevich
Chief Marketing Officer at Ware Malcomb

"'Trust me, I'm honest and authentic.' Unfortunately, it isn't so easy. Trust must be earned over time through complete transparency—in good times and bad. Social media will expose inconsistencies and spin with a single tweet. However, individuals and brands that recognize the wisdom of the crowd and communicate in an honest and authentic manner will be rewarded with powerful advocates."

Will Seccombe
Chief Marketing Officer at VISIT FLORIDA

"Establishing trust in social media is job one. You do it by sharing great content, giving proper credit, joining in conversations, and when you don't know, say so. The time and persistent effort it takes yields great rewards. You help others and, in turn, make new friends, generate ideas, and cultivate opportunities."

Barbara Price
Chief Marketing Officer at Mercer Capital

"By now, we all know the way to establish trust in social media is to be authentic and use your own voice, not just the voice of the brand. Since we live in a world in which we can no longer control the message, we should ask questions, encourage comments, and even admit mistakes. This also means no ghost blogging or tweeting. The demands of authenticity and engagement in social media have helped to change cultures inside companies. Social media has taught us the power of being responsive, credible, and people-centric."

Jonathan Becher
Chief Marketing Officer at SAP

"Today's sports fans have a powerful voice as both consumers of the products and services that sponsor their favorite sports as well as with the sports properties themselves. The fans invest time, money, and emotional energy into both the sports and the endorsers. Social media is a way to directly connect constituent-fans in a real-time manner with insider information tailored just for them. This is a chance for sports properties and their sponsors to 'direct connect' with the ultimate voice of success or failure of their sports marketing campaigns. The best sports properties get it right with insightful, honest, and can't-buy social media information. That information must be honest while remaining true to the team's brand and sponsors. Such honesty and insight builds trust and stickiness in a fan base, and that's a recipe for lifetime fan/consumer loyalty for sports properties. Social media provides sports properties a more intimate fan engagement opportunity, and leading sports properties are leveraging this to the benefit of their organizations—which now include a new 'insider:' the constituent-fan."

John Lopes
Chief Marketing Officer at Andretti Autosport

WHAT INNOVATIVE MARKETING BOOK AUTHORS HAVE TO SAY ABOUT THE MANDATE TO "ESTABLISH TRUST"

"The hardest part of establishing trust in social media, as with anything, is consistency. Reaching out with relevance and starting a relationship is exciting and fun. It provides a rush like the dating scene, and we rack up followers and feel important, smart, and loved. But like a marriage or long-term relationship of lasting value, trust in social media comes from consistency, particularly in regard to follow up. Did you send the URL to the article a friend asked for? Did you reach out to RT a client just because you liked their quote versus just sucking up? For trust to stick, here's some advice—worry less about the volume of followers you have and more about the ways you delight a chosen set you really want to build value for. Remember, they're the ones who will decide to trust you—the actions you take will demonstrate you're worthy of their commitment to do so."

John C. Havens
Co-Author of *Tactical Transparency: How Leaders Can Leverage Social Media to Maximize Value and Build their Brand*

"Without first earning trust, you really cannot earn social capital. Without social capital, what you attempt online will be just as difficult as wandering a foreign city without even a coin of the local currency. Since you're a smart business person, you know better. You know to prepare properly if the journey is to be a success. "

Laura Fitton
Co-Author of *Twitter for Dummies*

"Failure to establish trust in social media—as in all forms of brand communication—is a deal breaker. But what is 'trust' in the context of brand? It's really 'confidence' that the brand can and will deliver on promises and expectations, and that it will do so consistently. Without it, you have nothing."

Rick Mathieson
Author of *The On-Demand Brand: 10 Rules for Digital Marketing Success in an Anytime, Everywhere World*

"In an age of corporate secrets, a little honesty and transparency go a long way toward building trust with your prospects and long-term commitment from your customers. Once you're committed to creating a presence in social media outlets, there's no going back, and you really have no choice but to embrace transparency. Just as we fall in love with people who can listen to us and we can trust, we fall in love with companies that can do the same."

Dave Kerpen
Author of *Likeable Social Media: How to Delight Your Customers, Create an Irresistible Brand, and Be Generally Amazing on Facebook (and Other Social Media Networks)*

"Establishing trust is critical to success in social media because social media is all about relationships—with your employees, vendors, and customers. As in any relationship, a high level of trust is absolutely key. People don't refer people to brands they don't trust. People don't pass along content from brands they don't trust. And people don't buy (repeatedly) from brands they don't trust. Trust is also key to brand reputation. Just ask BP. Or Nestle. Trust and goodwill built up over time are absolutely critical when managing your reputation in times of need. Untrustworthy actions may be tempting for short-term gains, but an untrustworthy action in social media lives on for a long time, is noticed by more than you think, tolerated by few, and stains your overall customer experience. Trust lays the groundwork for leads, referrals, and clicks."

Linda Ireland
Author of *Domino: How Customer Experience Can Tip Everything in Your Business toward Better Financial Performance*

"The key to online trust is reliance. People in life don't know what they like . . . they like what they know. Want to establish trust? Work toward continuously meeting your promises and exceeding customer expectations."

Stan Phelps
Author of *What's Your Purple Goldfish? How to Win Customers and Influence Word of Mouth*

WHAT INNOVATIVE MARKETING PROFESSORS HAVE TO SAY
ABOUT THE MANDATE TO "ESTABLISH TRUST"

"We now live and work in a 'global village' with expansive social and business spheres. The underpinning technologies of the Internet, Web 2.0, and social media are enablers. Communication among people is the raison d'être— whether for personal or professional intent. Whom do you trust in your personal and professional spheres? Establishing trust is about consistency and credibility. The people who show up, are present, and are there for you day in and day out on a consistent, regular basis are trustworthy. The people who speak the truth, have reasoned thinking, have authority, and align themselves with other credible people are trustworthy. These same social behaviors are necessary constructs in the global village—powered by social media."

Michelle Corsano
Professor at the University of Toronto

"To trust someone is an emotional decision. And trust must be earned. Because of the virtual nature of social media, true engagement will only occur when there is some level of trust between parties. Online or offline, trust doesn't originate from perfect behavior; rather, it comes from demonstrating responsibility. So always honor your commitments by doing what you say you will do, respond promptly to inquiries, and be sincere and transparent at all times. Doing so will engender positive feelings about you and a sense of trust from those you associate with on social media—and in life."

Joaquin Presas
Professor at UniBrasil

"Social media implies a process of value co-creation with customers and/or consumers: interactions, expectations, and sharing ideas, content, solutions, or complaints. All this leads to a fair value distribution among stakeholders. But without establishing trust, the whole endeavor becomes suspicious."

Eric Vernette
Professor at the Université de Toulouse

"In the social media environment, where information overload increases the difficulty of processing that information, trust is essential. It allows you to break through the clutter and develop stronger bonds with friends, colleagues, and even brands. And by building trust systematically, you can create a solid foundation for strong consumer engagement as well."

Christophe Benavent
Professor at Université Paris Ouest

"Trust on social media platforms acts as a type of currency, since it's the basis for social media engagement and interaction. As a result, trust must be earned every day in everything you do as an individual or as an organization. To this end, it's important to provide strong products and services, be transparent in your relationships, and communicate consistently in your messaging."

Heidi Cohen
Adjunct Professor at Rutgers University

"Without trust, relationships will not move forward. In fact, I often think of building trust through this formula: Trust = (Rapport x Credibility) / Risk. Increase rapport and credibility while reducing risk, and watch trust grow! In the global economy, we read plenty about establishing customer trust; however, you don't see too much written about trusting the customer. Can you earn trust without giving it? Not when it comes to social media. Two-way trust is what makes transparent conversations possible. And transparent conversations move relationships forward."

Alan See
Associate Professor at the University of Phoenix

Frontier Airlines

The Organization

Currently in its 18th year of operation, Frontier Airlines employs more than 5,500 aviation professionals and operates more than 500 daily flights from its hubs at Denver International Airport, Milwaukee's General Mitchell International Airport, and Kansas City International Airport. Frontier offers service to more than 80 destinations in the United States, Mexico, and Costa Rica.

The Challenge

When a nasty hail storm hit Denver International Airport in the summer of 2011, it severely damaged 22 of Frontier's planes. That meant thousands of its customers would immediately face flight cancellations and lengthy delays. And that would most likely result in an uproar on social media.

The Solution

In order to help quickly reduce negative sentiment and bolster trust, the Frontier social media team proactively disseminated information through various social channels, including Twitter and Facebook. Using Radian6 to track down mentions of Frontier all across the social web, the social media staff assisted the reservations group with reaching out to customers to re-book flights, communicate up-to-date information, and let them know that Frontier was there to help.

The Results

The first few days following the storm were challenging, but soon the social media team at Frontier saw an increase in the "thank you" tweets. And because of the quick action taken by its staff, Frontier was able to connect with more than 4,000 customers over a seven-day period, and during that time saw more than 700,000 visitors to the company's Facebook page. Most importantly, Frontier was able to retain the level of customer trust that the airline had worked so hard to build over the past two decades.

Submitted by Sarah Carver, Product Marketing Manager–Customer Stories at Radian6

Calla Gold

The Organization

Located in Santa Barbara, California, Calla Gold is a personal jeweler—a "jeweler without walls"—who takes pride in working with clients one on one to integrate their personal sense of style and taste into custom-designed jewelry and repaired jewelry pieces.

The Challenge

Calla has operated her personal jeweler business for more than 25 years. She built it using classic marketing techniques, such as advertising, networking, and offering stellar service to build a loyal clientele. But a "jeweler without walls" (she doesn't have a storefront) can lack the credibility factor that brick and mortar competitors enjoy. As a result, potential clients were more likely to trust traditional jewelers and take their business there.

The Solution

To help overcome that roadblock to expanding her business, Calla hired Web Marketing Therapy (WMT), a boutique agency that specializes in marketing strategy. Guided by Stanford University's web credibility guidelines, Calla and WMT worked together to design and launch a new social-centric website, e-book, blog, Facebook page, and YouTube channel for Calla Gold that placed a strong emphasis on building trust via professional design, clear messaging, compelling educational content, and several other key factors.

The Results

Calla has evolved from using a "push marketing" model (buying expensive ads and having to hard sell clients on why she was as trustworthy as the big-box jewelry stores) to a "pull marketing" model (where Calla's online properties all work together to generate leads and build trust before people even call her). Blog and Facebook posts, social comments, videos, photo sharing, and a new social media strategy have elevated the business to a whole new level. Calla Gold's close rate has gone from 25% to 75%, and the average order amount and overall revenues have increased dramatically as well.

Submitted by Lorrie Thomas Ross, CEO of Web Marketing Therapy

Vistage International

The Organization

Founded in 1957, Vistage International is the world's leading peer advisory membership organization, serving more than 15,000 CEOs and senior executives in 15 countries. Vistage members participate in advisory board peer groups, receive one-to-one coaching, learn from expert speakers, and interact among a global network of CEOs representing a broad range of industries. Its renowned Vistage CEO Confidence Index has been tracking CEO confidence and "Main Street" business issues since 2003.

The Challenge

Vistage started a corporate blog entitled "The Vistage Buzz Blog" in April 2010 in order to create a voice for Vistage outside of its already established community. But six months after the launch, growth topped out around 2,000 unique visitors per month, because the content looked like it was coming from an organization instead of a trusted source.

The Solution

Vistage took down all of its branding on the blog and rebranded it "Executive Street." The focus of the blog shifted from content provided by Vistage and its community to content provided by a number of thought leaders from multiple facets of the business world. The organization also formed content partnerships with American Express Open Forum and prominent bloggers such as Chris Brogan, Amy Porterfield, Terry Starbucker, and Cameron Herold. Through these newly formed relationships and unbiased content, Vistage established a higher level of trust with its readership.

The Results

Since Vistage rebranded its blog as Executive Street, unique monthly visitors have grown from 2,000 to more than 15,000. Not only has the organization established a voice outside of its community, but the revamping of the blog has also resulted in the acquisition of new members who may not have previously experienced the Vistage brand.

Submitted by Benji Hyam, Social Media Coordinator at Vistage International

RiseSmart

The Organization

RiseSmart is a Silicon Valley startup that offers next-generation outplacement solutions. The company employs a cloud-based technology platform, proprietary job-matching software, and proven methodologies to deliver highly personalized job leads and other job search tools to workers in transition.

The Challenge

Since its top executives came from other industries, RiseSmart entered the close-knit world of human resources management as an outsider. Its technology-driven offering also ran counter to the traditional outplacement service model offered by the large, established players that had dominated the industry for decades. It was imperative to build brand recognition, authority, and trust for RiseSmart while ensuring that the company's business model was effectively communicated to key audiences.

The Solution

Social media use had been at the heart of RiseSmart's integrated content marketing strategy since its founding in 2007. The company's first authority-building initiative was the development of the "Career 100," an algorithm-based system for ranking the influence of HR and career blogs that attracted significant interest across the blogosphere. RiseSmart promoted the Career 100, as well as its own blog, by engaging followers on Twitter, and it ultimately emerged as an up-and-coming provider of B2B outplacement solutions.

The Results

RiseSmart is now widely recognized as one of the most followed and trusted influencers in the HR category. Other top industry influencers post comments on the company's blog and re-tweet its online conversations. RiseSmart's success in building trust in the HR community has helped it to win Fortune 500 clients away from more established competitors and grow its annual revenues by more than 700% over the past four years.

Submitted by Scott Baradell, Founder and President of the Idea Grove

Mandate #5:
Demonstrate Leadership

Social media leaders—as is the case with their offline counterparts—are most often valued and respected for their knowledge, experience, passion, and vision. The most effective social media leaders also demonstrate a strong sense of responsibility, serve as standard bearers, have a relatively high tolerance for risk, lead by example, think strategically, plan for the short and long term, express humility, and have the innate ability to inspire others.

Another important characteristic synonymous with social media leadership is integrity—and because of the ability for others to quickly and easily spot insincerity and dishonesty on social media, a leader's integrity must be solid as a rock at all times.

Innovation is another hallmark of a strong leader. The most successful leaders on social media not only create new concepts and trends and serve as change agents, they also figure out unique ways to generate value and generously and consistently share that value with their online communities.

Are you an influencer? Every effective social media leaders is. In fact, many of their friends and followers are subconsciously looking to be influenced. It's how they learn. And that's why they keep coming back to the leaders for guidance and inspiration.

Finally, what about leadership style? Think about those leaders you know who are akin to a tyrant straddling a big black stallion. Or the other ones you know who are compassionate but have a firm hand on their ship's tiller and wise words of advice for their shipmates. Which approach do you think has the most impact in the social media world?

Demonstrating leadership is probably the fastest way to create a loyal following on social media. But along with that comes responsibility. So take it seriously.

WHAT INNOVATIVE CHIEF MARKETING OFFICERS HAVE TO SAY ABOUT THE MANDATE TO "DEMONSTRATE LEADERSHIP"

"For social media to work for you as a professional, you must decide to take the lead and be responsible to a group of people you care about. Once you define that group, you then build your social media execution around what that group wants and needs. Your blog posts revolve around their issues. Your own follows and digital searches focus on resources that your group will find helpful, insightful, and enlightening. And more than anything else, you are a consistent voice and model that your group looks forward to hearing from or accessing."

Allen Fuqua
Chief Marketing Officer at Winstead

"Innovation is the fuel that powers leadership in the social media revolution."

Mark Addicks
Chief Marketing Officer at General Mills

"The greatest attribute of social media is that it enables corporate transparency. As such, to succeed, you must allow your network to freely share its views while ensuring your content is creative and relevant. To be a social media leader, you must do just that—lead. Develop a plan and a set of goals, engage a network of messengers, and maintain a legally sound social media policy unique to your organization."

Nina Buik
Chief Marketing Officer at HP's Connect Worldwide

"The key anchors of social media are influence and persuasion. Demonstrating inspirational leadership is essential to influencing and persuading others to act. To lead also means to set a pathway for execution. In social media, great execution is the ultimate differentiator."

Margaret Molloy
Chief Marketing Officer at Velocidi

"The most effective way to lead in social media is from the front. Social media is inherently . . . social. To truly seize the opportunity, leaders must actively participate, experiment, learn, connect, and above all, share thoughts. Standing on the sidelines will not take you or your organization very far."

Dan Marks
Chief Marketing Officer at First Tennessee Bank

"Demonstrating leadership in social media marketing means knowing the value of being 'first,' versus the 'best.' Ultimately, you want to lead your company to be the best at any marketing strategy you pursue, but there are times when you should be the innovator—a pioneer—and just jump in first to experiment and become an early participant of a new social channel. Other times, you may want to let the channel mature a little and then swoop in. Depending on your company's business model and target audience, you are a leader when you can distinguish which approach will drive the greatest value for your company. Demonstrating leadership involves not only sharing valuable content, creating interactive dialogue, and stimulating long-term positive brand affinity, but it is also managing when, where, and how you participate."

Jim Arnold
Chief Marketing Officer at MetricsBoard

"In the world of social media, there is no substitute for doing. Too many leaders think that their PowerPoint slides and a vision equal leadership. But true leaders demonstrate their leadership every day by actually engaging in social media. They are quick to comment on a blog post, tweet, or update on Facebook. They are willing to try a new sharing app, upload their presentations to SlideShare, and be part of the never-ending conversation. Their organizations are watching them. They need to lead by example."

Brian Kardon
Chief Marketing Officer at Lattice Engines

WHAT INNOVATIVE MARKETING BOOK AUTHORS HAVE TO SAY ABOUT THE MANDATE TO "DEMONSTRATE LEADERSHIP"

"To impact using social media going forward, it is necessary to first be focused on what the audience is interested in and wants to talk about, and second, to be creative in providing content. The key is to trigger community involvement by providing new information like BettyCrocker.com, entertaining like RedBull.com, having compelling promotions like P&G, or connecting to common interests like PampersVillage.com. All this will only happen to brands that lead, that get out in front."

Dr. David Aaker
Author of *Brand Relevance: Making Competitors Irrelevant*
and *Spanning Silos: The New CMO Imperative*

"You will attract more followers digitally in two days than you will in two months if you show interest in them versus trying to get them interested in you. This is what digital leadership is all about, and it is essential for social influence and success."

Erik Qualman
Author of *Socialnomics: How Social Media Transforms the Way We Live and Do Business* and *Digital Leader: 5 Simple Keys to Success and Influence*

"The shrill, noisy, and extemporaneous nature of the social web is not exactly an ideal environment for leadership. I think this is one of the reasons true leaders stand out so very brilliantly in this arena. Even though any kind of "rules" or hierarchy are disdained on the web, people have an innate urge to want to know who is in charge—even when nobody is in charge! Too much credit is placed today in social proof "badges" like Twitter followers and Klout scores. I sense that people are hungry for real leaders to step up and establish a voice of authority, communicate calmly and clearly, and show others how to make sense of this chaotic world. "

Mark Schaefer
Author of *The Tao of Twitter: Changing Your Life and Business 140 Characters at a Time*

"Social media is cluttered with 'experts,' 'gurus,' and 'leaders'—all claiming unique knowledge, insight, and vision into what has come before and what will be. The problem with all these 'experts' is that few truly are. Demonstrating leadership on social media requires a commitment to authenticity, transparency, and collaboration. Just telling me you are a guru, without proof or validation, is simply marketing. Instead, show your expertise through collaboration, demonstrate your knowledge by writing and speaking about insightful issues, and live your leadership claim by making bold promises and consistently delivering against expectations. True leadership in social media requires humility, genuineness, and a passion for engaging with others to create better outcomes, discussions, and ideas. Be the vision. Demonstrate leadership. The world of social media will reward your efforts with credibility—and that's priceless."

Lida Citroën
Author of *Reputation 360: Creating Power through Personal Branding*

"In order to build a large, loyal following on any of the popular social channels, you need to be 'followable.' One of the most powerful ways of doing so is to only ever share handpicked, quality content with your network. Over time, you'll become known as a top content curator and a trusted, go-to source within your industry. When you've built up this trust within your community, you have the ability to lead your network to the best resources—people will trust whatever you endorse. I believe the larger your community grows, the greater the responsibility you have to lead your followers with the utmost professionalism, mutual respect, and integrity, and this ultimately creates more success for you and for them."

Mari Smith
Co-Author of *Facebook Marketing: An Hour a Day*

WHAT INNOVATIVE MARKETING PROFESSORS HAVE TO SAY ABOUT THE MANDATE TO "DEMONSTRATE LEADERSHIP"

"Thought leaders in marketing must do more than talk about new media. Academics and practitioners must be early adopters of every iteration of the pull wave. Our integrity as leaders depends upon our active engagement. Engagement goes beyond sticking our toes in the water. Social media removes all excuses for trial that were inherent in broadcast media. Production costs, airtime, and continuity made learning and experimentation nearly prohibitive. We can accelerate the evolution of social media by total immersion into the wave. And a new generation of marketers will watch, learn, and launch their own wave."

Dr. Steve Greene
Professor at Oral Roberts University

"'Business as usual' is no longer an operating mantra for companies and individuals. Although social media is disruptive in how people communicate, discover, and share, it is above all for me as an educator an incredibly valuable tool for learning. Leadership on social media comes from demonstrating early adoption, innovation, opening doors, exploring boundaries, and adapting to change, toward inspiring students on a new route to success in a culture of connectivity, experimentation, and advanced learning."

John Heuston
Professor at City of Glasgow College

"A world awash with options creates both opportunity and anxiety. Confident leadership is an antidote to anxiety. It frees others to be more focused, flexible, and creative—and that's what's required to fearlessly face the wild west frontier otherwise known as social media marketing."

Kit Yarrow
Professor at Golden Gate University

"Social media is about conversations, interactions, and experiences that influence us more than technology and business. In the right hands and with strong leadership, it's a powerful communication tool."

Dr. Luc Dupont
Professor at the University of Ottawa

"Before there was 'social media,' there was a public conversation—led by writers and artists, protestors and politicians, scientists and social workers, advertisers and advocates. People who created change through the power of ideas. People whose words and actions motivated millions. The public conversation is alive and well—and being fueled by social media. Not necessarily by making wisecracks in 140 characters or less (although it can happen)! But just as the public conversation has always been influenced by leaders with ideas, imagination, and dedication, social media success depends on those very same factors. Because people who can lead in social media can also lead the public conversation—and that is where real change can happen.

Johanna Skilling
Adjunct Professor at New York University

"Effective leadership on social media is always accompanied by a personal touch that extends beyond the corporate brand. However, successful leaders also understand that their personal brand must reflect their organization's DNA. Every action, every message, every input should have the unmistakable essence of the brand, as that is what most often attracts and influences others."

Roberto Arancibia
Professor at the Universidad UNIACC , Universidad del Pacífico, and Universidad Mayor

Kimberly-Clark

The Organization

Kimberly-Clark and its well-known global brands are an indispensable part of life for people in more than 175 countries. Every day, nearly one quarter of the world's population trust its products and solutions to enhance their health, hygiene, and well-being. With brands such as Kotex, Kleenex, Scott, Huggies, Pull-Ups, and Depend, Kimberly-Clark holds number one or number two share positions in more than 80 countries.

The Challenge

Kotex, one of Kimberly-Clark's hallmark brands, wanted to support its tagline—"Your period is as unique as you are"—and publicly recognize that each woman is a unique individual with her own personality, way of life, and style. But how could the brand help women express themselves freely and openly, emphasizing style and design?

The Solution

With the help of Smoyz, a creative advertising agency in Israel, Kotex exhibited leadership and innovation on social media by running what it claims is the first-ever Pinterest marketing campaign in the world, dubbed "Women's Inspiration Day." The strategy involved targeting 50 influential Pinterest users and taking the time to understand what they pinned—and therefore, what interested them. Kotex and Smoyz brought each of those 50 woman's inspirations to life by creating a customized box of gifts based on her "pins." To receive their gifts, all each woman had to do was "re-pin" the image of the gifts she was to receive from Kotex.

The Results

After the gifts were delivered straight to their doorsteps, nearly 100% of the 50 recipients "pinned" their gift onto Pinterest, tweeted about it on Twitter, and/or posted about it on Facebook and Instagram, leading to 2,284 interactions and 694,853 total impressions for the Kotex brand.

Submitted by Michael Litman, Head of Engagement at 90:10 Group

Bayer Advanced

The Organization

Bayer Advanced is a leading consumer lawn and garden brand. The company offers a variety of proprietary chemicals to customers for residential use in the beautification and protection of their homes and yards—delivering fast action and long-lasting results.

The Challenge

More than 40% of shoppers leave the lawn and garden aisles empty-handed and confused. This audience, however, is constantly clamoring for advice and guidance, especially on the issue of which product to use. Bayer Advanced wanted the ability to engage in ongoing dialogue with consumers, demonstrate leadership to them, and ensure they found the right product or combination of products for their individual home or garden needs.

The Solution

Jumping into dialogues with consumers via social media wasn't an immediate option for Bayer Advanced, whose products are highly regulated and potentially dangerous to people if not used properly. But under the guidance of Luckie & Company, Bayer Advanced established official social media policies and guidelines to mitigate risk. Then Luckie worked with the brand's various product groups to grow its fan and follower base on Facebook and Twitter through sponsored content, customer service, gardening tips, and rose-growing contests, culminating in a Rose Bowl Parade grand prize and tweet-up.

The Results

Bayer Advanced has made significant inroads with its core audience online. This key group of brand advocates has grown to almost 50,000 strong, more than all the competing brands' Facebook fans combined. The company's leadership on social media provides a powerful competitive advantage as well. Bayer Advanced now has a way to more deeply engage and cultivate its most valuable customers, coupled with the ability to activate them to amplify their love of the brand across the ever-growing social landscape.

Submitted by John Heenan, Chief Marketing Officer at Luckie & Company

Emerson Process Management

The Organization

Emerson Process Management provides automation technologies and expertise in industry-specific engineering, consulting, project management, and maintenance services to global process manufacturers in various industries, including chemical, oil and gas, refining, pulp and paper, power, food and beverage, pharmaceutical, and others.

The Challenge

Process manufacturers that were building larger, more complex, and more remote plants were increasingly relying on the automation suppliers to provide expertise throughout the lifecycle of the plant—from initial design through ongoing operations and maintenance. Known primarily for its strong product brands, Emerson needed to lift the accessibility and findability of its experts around the globe to help position the company as a thought leader in the industry.

The Solution

Six years ago, Emerson began increasing the visibility of its experts, initially through blogs and then through participation in various social media avenues. The company began with Facebook pages and groups, LinkedIn groups, and Twitter, and it ultimately developed an online community which extended an annual global customer event to be online 24x7x365. The blogs featured experts relaying stories of how issues were solved. By making these experts more accessible in blog posts and community discussion threads, thought leadership was firmly established and then expanded over time.

The Results

Unique visits to the blogs and communities grew by 42% and 225% respectively, and multi-million dollar opportunities have been identified and brought into the sales process by people connecting with the experts. Emerson is now seen as the social media leader in its industry and frequently shares best practices and lessons learned at industry events.

Submitted by Jim Cahill, Head of Social Media at Emerson Process Management

BioClinica

The Organization

BioClinica provides comprehensive clinical trial design and management solutions and services to pharmaceutical, biotechnology, and medical device providers. The company has supported more than 2,000 studies in all phases of clinical trial development and a broad range of therapeutic areas.

The Challenge

Search engine algorithms—such as Google Panda—continue to place more emphasis on the quantity, quality, and shareability of content within social media. And successfully building thought leadership and brand awareness on the web requires continuous focus on a 360-degree digital marketing plan. The BioClinica executive team was aware of that, and they also realized they would need to demonstrate leadership and constantly refine the quality of leads generated from BioClinica's digital marketing strategies by using a variety of search engine, social media, lead generation, and measurement tools.

The Solution

With strategic guidance from its digital marketing agency Find and Convert, BioClinica initiated a B2B content strategy with a highly specialized blog targeted at its niche industry. The company also got more involved in social media by sharing content from the new blog. Through Find and Convert, BioClinica even began conducting social media training webinars on digital marketing best practices, in order to teach its employees how to regularly share and promote content through their individual social profiles.

The Results

More than a year later, BioClinica continues to refine its leadership and content strategy, based on industry changes and new industry buzzwords. Social media mentions are up more than 200%, and BioClinica is now in a hiring mode to keep up with all the business generated in part through its digital marketing initiatives.

Submitted by Bernie Borges, Founder and CEO of Find and Convert

Mandate #6:

Build Community

Building a loyal community of fans and followers is not a snap-your-finger deal. You have to put the "right stuff" out there to attract and grow an audience, and you'll have to continually nurture the crop before it bears any fruit. But the payoff for that investment can be significant.

Where to begin, you ask? Start by identifying key influencers and cultivating individual relationships with them that you can later aggregate into a group of people who share common interests. This is your foundation—the heartbeat of your social media marketing activity. These relationships will become the core of your community and will help you expand its reach and contribute to its growth and influence.

The key to aggregation is providing quality content to your community that interests your target audience—content that's informational in nature, not a sales pitch. And make sure that content is always relevant to your strategy and your followers. Effective connections with your audience are built when you provide information that's based on understanding your market segment and your community's needs, and by presenting those relevant morsels in a concise, easy-to-digest way.

And make it easy for your community members to share your content with their other communities. This will help dramatically expand your reach. Also, you don't have to create all the content yourself; instead, promote the submission of user content from within your community, so everyone who wants to get involved is able to do so.

Yes, community building can be difficult, mainly because it requires determination, dedication, and grit—and a lot of time. But it's key to your longevity in social media.

WHAT INNOVATIVE CHIEF MARKETING OFFICERS HAVE TO SAY ABOUT THE MANDATE TO "BUILD COMMUNITY"

"Don't try to reinvent the social web. Brands should integrate with their customers' existing social communities instead of creating standalone communities—'build it and they will come' isn't the way the social web works. Build your customers' existing social networks into your site to create a seamless experience that gives them the opportunity to interact with each other—and you—in a branded context."

Erin Nelson
Chief Marketing Officer at Bazaarvoice

"We want our customers to engage and experience a sense of belonging when they are doing business with us, a real connection to our brand."

John Jacko
Chief Marketing Officer at Kennametal

"From our early days of social media at AMD, it was clear that it was about two things—conversations and communities. When we were being most successful, we were having the right conversation with the community of people who cared. When the message strayed out of our community into another, the message was less successful. The right message, however, both strengthened our community or ecosystem and quickly built additional value for itself by amplifying it."

Nigel Dessau
Chief Marketing Officer at AMD

"The market—your customers, prospects, influencers, competitors—are having conversations about you already. Building a community helps you encourage, monitor, participate, and even shape the dialogue. If you are authentic, responsive, and engaging, the community will reward you with insights for better innovation, retention, and expansions."

Tim Minahan
Chief Marketing Officer at Ariba

"Let's face it, not all online content is good, and only a handful is really great. Once your social media community starts generating great content, it's smart to reuse it across as many platforms as possible. While syndication is crucial, community content has real value, because you know it has value to the customer. That intersection of business and customer value is where you break through the noise and make memorable connections."

Karen Quintos
Chief Marketing Officer at Dell

"Whether you build your own community or 'rent' one from a provider like LinkedIn (Groups), a community is a great place to discuss your services or solutions with your existing customers. B2B marketers often host advisory board and user group meetings, and these forums are hungry to stay connected via a tool like an online community. When you do that, the results reported in a recent Jive report of more than 2,000 customers are outstanding. Lower costs and increased revenue—a perfect combination!"

Paul Dunay
Chief Marketing Officer at Networked Insights

"Building community is critical to success in today's business environment. Community enables organizations to be directly in touch with the voice of the customer at what is potentially the greatest listening post that brands have ever known. An active and engaged community offers insights that benefit product design, pricing, competitive positioning, service offerings, and brand sentiment. I believe so strongly in the power of engaged community that I have established the BHAG (big, hairy, audacious goal)of 'never having to advertise for a lead again.' Our community spans the spectrum from awareness to advocacy and scales in a manner that would otherwise be impossible to achieve."

Rod Brooks
Chief Marketing Officer at PEMCO Mutual Insurance

WHAT INNOVATIVE MARKETING BOOK AUTHORS HAVE TO SAY ABOUT THE MANDATE TO "BUILD COMMUNITY"

"Social media is just that—social. It doesn't work if you approach it as just another sales tool or transactional contact method like a call center. The main reason is that your audience has to agree to get your message. Since you are not—as in the case of TV or radio—subsidizing the cost of their access to the medium, the only currency that matters to the target audience is content and community. Successful community builders should see themselves as hosting an elite social gathering—the guest list and venue, frequency of meeting, anchor names, and conversation are crucial. Instead of canapes and champagne, you have to provide an endless supply of excellent content and insight. And just as it would be a social disaster to sell at a classy cocktail party, you have to wait for your audience to ask how they can buy from you."

Jessie Paul
Author of *No Money Marketing: From Upstart to Big Brand on a Frugal Budget*

"During the last two years alone, we witnessed Verizon, Gap, HP, Chrysler, ESPN, and Go Daddy all reverse courses, pushed to change policies and proclamations by a groundswell of customer dissatisfaction using today's instant technologies—social, mobile, and cloud—that impact business decisions. Verizon's ill-conceived $2 fee for one-time online payments didn't survive 24 hours, Netflix's pricing change cost it billions in shareholder value, and the Gap had to reverse its logo and new branding in less than a month. In short, readily available social, mobile, and cloud technologies empower customers, as well as employees, to take matters into their own hands and create unprecedented new risks for boards, leaders, and their organizations. The only solution: organizations need to build customer and employee communities that enable leaders to fully understand what their stakeholders want—and then deliver it to them."

Barry Libert
Author of *Social Nation: How to Harness the Power of Social Media to Attract Customers, Motivate Employees, and Grow Your Business*

"Online communities create the opportunity for synergies between you, your brand, and others in a way that complements each element of individual skill and experience, in turn, creating a valuable mix of those who work together most effectively. By sharing valuable information with your community, rather than going down the 'hard-sell' route, you are, in effect, educating its members about what you do and what you offer by allowing them to get to know you on a personal as well as professional level. It's all about trust!"

Dr. Dean Anthony Gratton
Co-Author of *Zero to 100,000: Social Media Tips and Tricks for Small Businesses*

"Social communities are the new 'keeping up with the Joneses.' For example, enabling a car buyer to notify his community that he bought a new BMW is more credible, and it triggers more status-seeking responses than directly advertising to members of the community itself."

Adrian Ott
Author of *The 24-Hour Customer: New Rules for Winning in a Time-Starved, Always-Connected Economy*

"Having spent the last 15 years of my life building communities, both online and off, I realize that it is arguably one of the most important things we can do in business. Some people call it networking, but I think 'community-building'—or creating deep engagement and value with those who are important to you across a variety of interests, professional and personal—is the only way to succeed in life."

Aaron Strout
Co-Author of *Location-Based Marketing for Dummies*

WHAT INNOVATIVE MARKETING PROFESSORS HAVE TO SAY ABOUT THE MANDATE TO "BUILD COMMUNITY"

"Modern society is a lonely place, and one response to this has been the growth of communities around activities and products. In many instances, we call these new communities 'consumer tribes.' Companies have started to respond with factory visits, clubs, limited editions, and stores more like art galleries. With social media now an essential part of everyday life for so many consumers, they expect to be able to interact in this space with their favorite brands. A company must respond if it wants to be to be relevant and informed. And a clever company is one that is willing to dialogue and intermingle with its loyal customers, rather than broadcast to them. It is a case of losing a little control to gain a lot of loyalty."

Mike Redwood
Professor at the University of Bath

"On social media, building community is important because it unites like-minded individuals around a shared purpose. Members of the community can then share ideas and tips for more effective use of the product or introduce solutions to other members' common problems. Building community can give your brand or product a distinct personality that is reflected by the members of the social network. Community members tend to be helpful and enthusiastic, traits which often can accrue to your own product."

Patrick Strother
Visiting Associate Professor at the University of Minnesota

"When used strategically to build community, social media empowers brands with the tools to listen, show appreciation, and connect with their audience on a real and sustainable level. As a result, the audience feels a sense of belonging and pride that ultimately leads to brand evangelism."

Dr. Bobbi Kay Lewis
Associate Professor at Oklahoma State University

"It is satisfying to publish one's thoughts, but the ultimate value of social media is the community. A group with complementary interests can focus on the worthy ideas and help generate more. Some ideas will be clearly crowdsourced or outsourced, but many will seem self-generated. A milestone success measure in building community is the realization that 'you' have become more creative and are generating more ideas!"

Dr. Gary Schirr
Assistant Professor at Radford University

"The digital world is also a beta world. Businesses and 'prosumers' are still in the learning phase, searching for better ways to address issues and solve problems. In this digital age, companies need to listen, be transparent, and truly relate to their prosumers—while also understanding how they behave on social networks. Creating online communities to take advantage of the great reach and influence of social media enables smart marketers to achieve significant results for their organizations."

Pedro Cordier
Professor at the Instituto Baiano de Ensino Superior

"Whether you are building your personal brand or creating an online environment for a client, it is imperative to build a community around your brand with social media. Building community will not only increase your exposure to like-minded individuals but also allow you to expand your customer relationship management efforts."

Dr. Laura Bright
Assistant Professor at Texas Christian University

Koodonation

The Organization

Koodo Mobile is Canada's smart and affordable wireless phone alternative. Launched in 2008, Koodo created a mobility revolution with its "decidedly different" approach to cellular service, featuring affordable, easy-to-understand plans that require no contracts or minimums and focus on what young Canadians want—talk, text, and social mobile.

The Challenge

Koodo wanted to create a new and meaningful social good movement for Canada's millennials by leveraging the social web. The company also wanted to inspire grassroots participation and give volunteers a say in where they spend their money and free time. But the process of making it easy, interactive, mobile, and social was daunting.

The Solution

Partnering with Toronto-based PR firm Strategic Objectives, Koodo created Koodonation, Canada's first-ever online microvolunteering community. Entirely not-for-profit and community driven, Koodonation has revolutionized volunteerism in Canada by enabling activities to be done entirely online, in small chunks of time. Member charities can login using their Facebook credentials or e-mail address to connect with social media influencers, news release writers, graphic designers, and a host of other talented volunteers who will help them with a variety of projects.

The Results

Koodonation has attracted volunteers and charities from coast to coast. Approximately 2,000 volunteers joined the Koodonation community in less than two months, and dozens more are signing up each day. In addition, more than 100 charities now post challenges/projects they need help with but don't have the expertise or budget to complete. Casie Stewart, one of Canada's most popular bloggers, volunteers as a Koodonation social ambassador. Koodonation has also been embraced by TEDx as an "idea worth spreading."

Submitted by Deborah Weinstein, President of Strategic Objectives

Cakes for Occasions

Organization

Cakes for Occasions in Danvers, Massachusetts is a boutique-style gourmet cake and pastry shop. Owner Kelly Delaney's mission is to create a defining moment for each of her customers through custom-designed cakes and unparalleled customer service.

Challenge

Cakes for Occasions had garnered quite a bit of traditional media attention, including being featured on the Today show, CNBC, and in *Gourmet* and *Yankee* magazines. But Kelly wanted to take her brand into the realm of social media, so she could continue to stay relevant and interact with her customers. She was faced with how, during a historically slow period (January), she could generate excitement and buzz while continuing to grow her social media community, with a particular focus on increasing her Facebook fan base.

Solution

Kelly launched a "Cakes for Occasions 2012 New Year Ambassador" contest that was promoted primarily through Facebook. To qualify, customers had to submit a photo of themselves with a Cakes for Occasions cake and a response to this: "Why I Deserve to Be the 2012 Cake Ambassador." Five finalists were chosen, and their entries were posted on the Cakes for Occasions Facebook page. The public voted for ("liked") their favorites. And of course, each finalist went to work soliciting votes from family and friends, posting the link on their own blogs and websites, and e-mailing colleagues with the link to the contest.

Results

Nearly 2,000 people voted in the poll, and the campaign generated a virality rating of 73%. The promotion also increased "likes" on the Cakes for Occasions page by 555% over regular activity for the campaign period and expanded Kelly's community on Facebook to more than 4,000 fans. The winner continues to spread the good word, enabling the Cakes for Occasions brand to stay top of mind.

Submitted by Sue Tabb, Senior Account Director at Thomson Communications

Cisco Support Community

The Organization

Since 2000, Cisco Support Community (CSC) has offered B2B community-based, peer-to-peer support for Cisco's enterprise, medium-sized, and small business customers across all Cisco product areas. CSC has grown exponentially—quadrupling in size over the last 18 months—and has become one of Cisco's most strategic channels for web-based support.

The Challenge

As CSC looked to engage with its next generation of customers around the world, it recognized social media as a significant opportunity for listening, having meaningful two-way conversations, providing technical support, and expanding its B2B communities.

The Solution

CSC launched new technical support channels on Facebook, Twitter, LinkedIn, Google+, and YouTube to build a more social and persistent community for peer-to-peer support. These new communities now provide direct access to Cisco experts to share knowledge, foster issue resolution among customers, and serve as vehicles for critical technical support announcements and updates from Cisco. CSC also launched a Facebook app to allow real-time, two-way integration of Facebook and the Cisco communities, allowing users to participate in those communities directly and seamlessly from Facebook.

The Results

CSC has been able to acquire, connect with, and engage more than 275,000 users with very minimal investments in tools, technologies, and personnel. It is likely to have an extended reach to more than 3,000,000 users worldwide as a result of Facebook's and Twitter's social graphs and network effect. And low-cost tools such as Sprinklr and Radian6 have made it less costly to manage and drive the growth on social media. According to a conservative estimate, CSC's community-based support on Facebook and Twitter is saving Cisco more than $1,000,000 annually, and this is expected to grow significantly over time.

Submitted by Pratibha Gupta, Senior Product Manager at Cisco Systems

Silicon Halton

The Organization

Silicon Halton is a grassroots, high-tech community of people who make a living, make meaning, and make things happen in technology in the Halton Region of Ontario, Canada. The community focuses on helping technology professionals and entrepreneurs connect, build relationships, and grow.

The Challenge

The Halton Region has a population of more than 500,000, spanning across 964 square kilometers. It is geographically situated between the Greater Toronto Area and Kitchener/Waterloo, both of which are technology hubs. Many technology professionals live and/or work in the region, but there was no technology hub or gathering place for them. There was also no local "technology scene" and very little opportunity to network and make connections, let alone start a new technology company.

The Solution

Founders Chris Herbert and Rich Stomphorst launched Silicon Halton by starting a private LinkedIn group and hosting monthly meetups where people in technology could gather, learn, and network. LinkedIn was the primary social media channel that was used to help build the geo/industry focused community and promote the gatherings. And the community was developed without any funding from members, government, or sponsors.

The Results

Silicon Halton now has more than 600 members representing more than 200 companies. There have been close to 50 meetups, with total attendance exceeding 1,000. There are five peer-to-peer groups for CEOs, solopreneurs, arts and tech enthusiasts, agile/lean professional developers, and iOS developers. As a result of relationships that have been started on LinkedIn and grown through Silicon Halton, numerous members are now generating new business, and at least two new companies have been formed.

Submitted by Chris Herbert, Co-Founder of Silicon Halton and Chief Marketing Officer at Mi6

Mandate #7:

Ensure Value

"What's the ROI from all that social media stuff you've been doing?" your boss asks. One of his favorite questions, right? Or if you're a small business owner, you've probably heard that same question from your partner or CPA.

Generating reliable performance metrics for your social media activities—gathered and reported in an efficient, easily interpreted manner—has become a major priority for practitioners of social media marketing to help them demonstrate the value from participating in social media and validate their investments in it.

Your boss, partner, or CPA wants to compare the investment of personnel, time, money, and other resources to the return. But without supplying verifiable ROI data and analysis, any long-term relationships that marketers hope to develop and maintain with their social media communities are most likely in jeopardy.

So how do you go about ensuring that you're deriving value from your social media marketing efforts—and that you can accurately measure that value? Obviously, tracking online "chatter" can help expose the bad as well as the good. For example, your fans and followers may publicly laud your products or suggest improvements to them, giving you the opportunity to respond quickly and address their comments or concerns. Also, there are now a myriad of technology tools available that can help measure the financial impact of social media on your organization, including lead generation, e-commerce revenue, etc.

The social media monitoring and measuring process is still in its infancy. However, in today's hyper-competitive environment and relatively weak economy, generating measurable, repeatable value from social media is no longer an option for most marketers.

WHAT INNOVATIVE CHIEF MARKETING OFFICERS HAVE TO SAY ABOUT THE MANDATE TO "ENSURE VALUE"

"In social media, we ask, 'Can we engage more users, and how do we measure it?' Engagement starts with an understanding of what users value and how to deliver it successfully. Time is the competition. That means we need to start by asking, 'Why is time spent with me more relevant than with someone else?' Value has to be exchanged for a user to engage. If we measure value, engagement will follow."

Beth Comstock
Chief Marketing Officer at GE

"Value is in the mind of the beholder, so one person's definition of value is, at best, an educated opinion based on experience. So to ensure value in social media is, at best, a concerted effort to think and act in such a way that you and your followers benefit from staying connected. This is achieved by sharing information and insights and having quality conversations that make it possible to strengthen your connections, relationships, and ultimately your own professional network. Value is generated by using social media to create and grow meaningful relationships with those people who matter to you and then showing how you can make a difference in helping them be successful."

Chris Herbert
Chief Marketing Officer at Mi6

"When it comes to providing value on social media, consider adopting an approach leveraging the 'Four Rs:' real-time relevance focused on remarkable ROI. Engagement is vital, yet social success today must also deliver usefulness. To know what is useful for your audience, learn what is relevant by leveraging analytics, optimization, and behavioral segmentation across all digital channels."

Hope Frank
Chief Marketing Officer at Webtrends

"The best way to ensure value is to find ways to transform the talk of social media into the action of social engagement. As Freud once said, the two most important things in life are love and work. After years of mostly idle chatter, social media is now enabling us to more effectively engage with people who want to get things done. A case in point: When designing the social strategy for the White House Initiative on Educational Excellence for Hispanics—a program that's crowdsourcing the development of educational opportunities for Hispanic youth—the program's leaders took care to make sure that citizens were involved in the work of the program, not just the communications. Not many organizations think this way, but the ones that do are making a difference."

Giovanni Rodriguez
Chief Marketing Officer at Deloitte Postdigital Enterprise

"Social media is sweeping the hearts and minds of many marketers. It strengthens the brand, helps companies build communities, and opens new possibilities for social commerce. Many are still wondering, however, when the value of social media can be realized as a fully scalable channel. Marketers have a challenging responsibility to show that the value of social media is far greater than an immediate conversion channel or a marketing campaign outlet. They need to be armed with metrics supported by the entire organization and with analytics exposing their assumptions and ambitions. Marketers also need to ensure the value to the organization and to the community around the brand, measured in visible success metrics and incentives for the community advocates. The value of social media needs to be clear and simplified—positive brand-related outcomes, paths to conversion, community incentives which are repeatable and appreciated, and clear evidence of positive sentiment growth."

Alex Romanovich
Chief Marketing Officer at Social2B

WHAT INNOVATIVE MARKETING BOOK AUTHORS HAVE TO SAY ABOUT THE MANDATE TO "ENSURE VALUE"

"For your social media efforts to cut through the clutter you MUST ensure value by consistently providing excellent content that is informing, entertaining, and interactive. Give your audience what they need, what they want, and what they can actually use. Stick to what you know and be honest about what you don't. This is the only way to ensure value and build relationships online—and in real life."

Eve Mayer Orsburn
Author of *The Social Media Business Equation: Using Online Connections to Grow Your Bottom Line*

"Nobody cares about your products and services except you. To ensure you deliver social media marketing of value, you must create content especially for your buyers. If you do focus on buyers, you'll beat the competition who are sitting on their butts in nice comfortable offices just making stuff up, which is the cause of most ineffective social media marketing. By truly understanding your buyer personas, you transform your social media marketing from mere product-specific, ego-centric gobbledygook that only you understand into valuable information people are eager to share via Facebook, Twitter, blogs, YouTube, and other networks. You brand your organization as one that's worthy of doing business with."

David Meerman Scott
Author of *The New Rules of Marketing and PR: How to Use News Releases, Blogs, Podcasting, Viral Marketing, and Online Media to Reach Buyers Directly*

"One of the most significant differences between traditional and social media marketing is that the latter is 100% permission based. I either choose to follow you, friend you, read your content . . . or not. And I make that choice every day. So if you don't offer me consistent value, I'm going to move on."

Drew McLellan
Author of *99.3 Random Acts of Marketing*

"It's so important to develop an empathetic bond with your followers and fans. Understanding their wants and needs will enable you to effectively gauge what content will add value by solving a problem, building credibility, and fostering trust. Remember that memory is tied to emotions and we, as humans, are continually governed by them on an unconscious level. Long-term brand awareness and loyalty is ultimately driven by these emotional ties which, in turn, are driven by the value we provide to others."

Dr. Sarah-Jayne Gratton
Co-Author of *Zero to 100,000: Social Media Tips and Tricks for Small Businesses*

"Ensuring value means more than just sharing what you're doing. People value resources, such as links to articles, offers, or whitepapers. And those resources must be tailored—appropriate for and valued by the social media audience being cultivated—and persistent. The savvy marketer queues up several tweets and Facebook updates per day. Guy Kawasaki has built up nearly 500,000 Twitter followers by tweeting about valuable and interesting resources every 15 minutes, with each tweet repeated four times per day. That's persistence!"

David Szetela
Co-Author of *Pay-per-Click Search Engine Marketing: An Hour a Day*

"Social media and blogging certainly enable us to give value to our customers through great information/content, but even more importantly, they enable us to share and express our values with them. Unlike the one-way communication of 'old school' marketing, we can now be known as real people, not just as businesses."

Lynn Serafinn
Author of *The 7 Graces of Marketing: How to Heal Humanity and the Planet by Changing the Way We Sell*

WHAT INNOVATIVE MARKETING PROFESSORS HAVE TO SAY ABOUT THE MANDATE TO "ENSURE VALUE"

"As marketers, we are all held accountable for our efforts, and social media marketing is no different. It's just a different channel that allows us to directly engage with our audiences and one in which we need to actively listen in order to be successful. Success should be defined by metrics, benchmarks, and goals. The metrics guide us (traffic to a website, number of shares on Facebook, how many times something is retweeted, etc.), and benchmarks help us actively pursue our goals and adjust our strategies in order to be successful. Measuring your social media marketing efforts is essential to ensuring there is value in what you are trying to accomplish."

Liana "Li" Evans
Adjunct Professor at Rutgers University

"Social media relationships are built on a foundation of trust and perceived value. While we may connect loosely with many people, our core connections are with those individuals and/or businesses that we perceive to provide added value. That is, core connections are based on our perception of the added value brought to the relationship by the business or person with whom we are connecting. Successful social media marketers strive to ensure value by systematically and consistently providing the resources desired by those connecting with them. A well-defined value proposition is the key to initiating a relationship built on value. While your value proposition may change over time, building on a solid foundation within one's area of expertise is a critical success factor for ensuring value in social media relationships."

Dr. Steve White
Professor at the University of Massachusetts at Dartmouth

"Inspiration, relevance, and originality are the building blocks to create valuable content, the most strategic variable to ensure traffic and increase influence."

Miguel Ángel Trabado
Associate Professor at the ESERP School of Business

"Social media provides new tools for marketers, but ensuring value requires following the old rules of human conversation. Conversations require taking turns and listening respectfully while the other person is speaking. Old broadcast media were one-way communication tools that made it easy for marketers to shout at customers but hard to listen to them. Social media are two-way communication tools that make it easy for organizations to talk to customers and for customers to talk to each other. Customers will value those organizations that listen and respond to their complaints, praise, and requests. They will tell their friends if they like you, which ensures even more value. Smart organizations will join the conversation and help build customer conversations and communities."

Dr. Raymond Fisk
Professor at Texas State University

"A good image and strong credibility have always been very important—not only for businesses but for those who work there as well. Companies and individuals who understand how to effectively create a positive image and build credibility can leverage them to add value to the conversation on social media. But if their products or services are sub-par, a social media presence, no matter how well thought out, can only go so far in enhancing the actual value that their company or personal brand can bring."

Beto Lima
Professor at Faculdades Integradas Hélio Alonso

"Consumers use social media over other channels because they expect better value in attention, interactivity, responsiveness, and information. The value you create and deliver through careful listening, friendly conversations, and effective solutions will determine your success in social media."

Dr. Bruce D. Weinberg
Professor at Bentley University

Wounded Warrior Project

The Organization

Wounded Warrior Project (WWP) is a nonprofit organization whose mission is to honor and empower Wounded Warriors—those who have incurred a service-connected injury on or after September 11, 2001. Offering a variety of programs and services, WWP is equipped to serve warriors with every type of injury—from the physical to the invisible wounds of war.

The Challenge

Warriors recover in communities around the globe, and this geographic dispersal made it impossible for WWP to provide in-person support. WWP needed a way to extend services and provide peer support to warriors, regardless of their location.

The Solution

WWP deployed a number of social channels to reach out to Wounded Warriors, their family members, and members of the general public who might know a warrior. The goal was to provide outreach, referrals, information, and peer support through tools such as Facebook, Twitter, YouTube, and a private online community for warriors called WWP Connect. WWP also decided to provide private, one-on-one outreach to warriors and family members whose posts mentioned that they were dealing with challenges.

The Results

WWP's online engagement program on Facebook has proven incredibly successful in assisting warriors and their families, most of whom were not aware they were eligible for the programs they desperately needed. Through WWP Connect, more than 3,000 warriors now encourage and help one another in their recoveries, and the privacy of the community fosters open conversations about intensely personal subjects and experiences. Additionally, WWP has empowered the public to participate in its mission. In the words of one warrior who received a WWP outreach message through Facebook, "It is so nice to know there are people who care out there! Keep up the wonderful work."

Submitted by Jen Boyce, Online Engagement Manager at Wounded Warrior Project

The Adolphus Hotel

The Organization

As the cherished standard for luxury accommodations since St. Louis beer baron Adolphus Busch opened its doors in 1912, The Adolphus is a baroque masterpiece that still stands today as the Grande Dame of downtown Dallas hotels. It's known as the place where "lone star legend meets four-diamond luxury."

The Challenge

The Adolphus wanted to better connect with its devoted guests while exposing the unique personality of the hotel to younger generations, most of whom were unaware of the "hip luxury" that awaited them. But The Adolphus management team also wanted to avoid the possibility of alienating the hotel's discerning, international client base and risk sacrificing its solid reputation.

The Solution

Working with Social Media Delivered, The Adolphus created added value for its fans and followers on social media with a heightened online presence on Facebook and Twitter. That value is now brought to life with extremely diverse, engaging, and highly interactive content focused on art, cuisine, travel, local history, pop culture, and other finer things in life that would appeal to its target audiences. For example, the hotel's Facebook page serves as an online lifestyle magazine full of "bite-sized" tidbits of entertaining, historical, and informative content, including beautiful photos and videos.

The Results

A passionate following of long-time guests and people experiencing the property for the first time began connecting through shared discussion. The Adolphus has become one of the most popular hotels on social media all around the world, with more than 3,000 "likes" on Facebook and more than 20,000 followers on Twitter. And for the first time in years, there has been a marked increase in new guests gracing the rooms of The Adolphus.

Submitted by David Davis, Director of Public Relations at the Adolphus Hotel

Adobe Photoshop

The Organization

Whether it's a smartphone or tablet app, a game, a video, a digital magazine, a website, or an online experience, chances are it was touched by Adobe technology. Adobe tools and services enable its customers to create groundbreaking digital content, deploy it across media and devices, and then continually measure and optimize it. Among Adobe's most popular products is the Photoshop family of software, which is used to bring out the best in digital images and has long been the market leader in its space.

The Challenge

Adobe wanted to encourage its brand advocates to share their love of Adobe products and provide real-time feedback online concerning the new versions of its Photoshop and Photoshop Extended software.

The Solution

Working with its marketing and technology partner Bazaarvoice, Adobe launched a ratings and reviews tool on the Adobe brand site. To also add value to its social community, Adobe simultaneously launched a Facebook counterpart, allowing the two million-plus Photoshop fans on Facebook to read and write reviews directly within the social network. It was also important to Adobe to listen and engage with the community in its social channels, so the company monitored the number of reviews collected and shared on Facebook. In addition, Adobe used A/B testing methods to measure the impact of ratings and reviews on actual conversions.

The Results

Adobe advocates rated both Photoshop and Photoshop Extended extremely high, with an average rating of 4.9 stars out of five. About 25% of the reviewers also shared their reviews via Facebook during the first week of the campaign—700% higher than the industry average. That influenced up to a 54% lift in page conversion on the Adobe brand site.

Submitted by Ian Greenleigh, Manager of Content and Social Strategy at Bazaarvoice

BearCom Wireless

The Organization

BearCom Wireless provides a broad line of high-performance wireless communications products, services, and complete mobility solutions. BearCom is America's only nationwide B2B dealer and integrator of wireless equipment, serves customers from 26 branch offices located throughout the United States, and has several affiliated offices around the world.

The Challenge

BearCom had been successful in building its brand and promoting its products and services with direct mail and e-mail campaigns, search engine optimization and pay-per-click programs, advertising, news releases, trade shows, and a variety of other traditional marketing tactics. But the sagging U.S. economy motivated company leaders to consider other options, including social media and content-based marketing.

The Solution

BearCom launched its social media platform on Twitter using @WirelessWoman to connect with its partners and the wireless industry and @BearCom to interact with its customers and prospects. The company also created the #WirelessWednesday movement to promote its newly formed Twitter community. Following its initial success on Twitter, BearCom expanded its social media presence with Facebook and LinkedIn pages, a YouTube channel that features animated videos starring Wireless Woman, and a blog. Most of the content the company has published is instructional in nature and is designed to help educate its constituents about how wireless technologies can enhance the success of their businesses.

The Results

BearCom now has more than 10,000 devoted fans and followers on social media. The company's success in adding value to its social media community has been featured on Computerworld.com and numerous wireless industry websites and blogs. Also, BearCom was nominated for a 2012 Twitter Shorty Award and ACBJ Social Madness Award.

Submitted by Nicki Nielsen, Marketing & PR Specialist at BearCom Wireless

Mandate #8:

Continue Listening

By Eric Fletcher

All listening is not created equal.

Consider how a physician uses the stethoscope in order to measure the activity of the human heart, or how a mother calibrates her ear to detect the faintest whimper of a newborn, or how a conductor trains the ear to pinpoint the one-out-of-a-hundred instruments slightly out of tune.

Compare these with the ability to tune out a barking dog, or half listen to the rant of a co-worker, or subconsciously mix the rhythm of the rain to the precise sleep-inducing decibel.

Now consider how we interpret tone, process innuendo, translate vernacular, and compose a whole new message—all while we (theoretically) listen in the context of conversation.

Indeed, all listening is not the same.

In order to discuss the role of listening in social media, we must first sort through the plethora of ways in which we engage in the act.

This Thing We Call Communication

Regardless of the venue—whether social media, conventional (mass) channels, or a much more intimate and personal setting, such as an office or living room—the art of communication is frequently reduced to the act of delivering a message.

When the subject is communicating, several names are notable, such as Ronald Reagan—dubbed the "Great Communicator," thanks to a charismatic and winning delivery. Or, staying for a moment with former presidents, the poetry of Abraham Lincoln's Gettysburg

Address and second inaugural are recognized as tapping into the heart and instigating vision in the midst of crisis. Writers like Shakespeare and Hemingway paint pictures so vivid they have come to life in multiple forms for centuries.

Today, those who are able to write, speak with clarity and ease, and master the mass media phenomenon of soundbites are thought to possess extraordinary communication skills. One able to coach corporate leaders, educators and politicians in the nuances of winning presentations is, in the vernacular, able to write her own ticket. Advertising copywriters, sitcom creators, and even pop novelists are sought after for their "ability to communicate."

Translation: we place high value on the art of message delivery.

In real and practical terms, we have come to equate the creation and delivery of a message with the whole of communication. And when the discussion turns to marketing—well, let's just say it is often about pumping up the volume: on the message and all that surrounds its delivery. From the Ringling Brothers to Apple's i-product introductions, marketing seems to focus on messaging.

So no one should be surprised that social media brought a whole new incarnation of the age-old question; what do we say, and how do we say it?

Bloggers everywhere began to wrestle with the significant challenge that often comes with regularly needing (or being expected to have) a message worth reading. Twitter offered momentary respite, if for no other reason than we only had to fill 140 characters. But the feeling of relief was short-lived once the real challenge set in: what can possibly be accomplished in 140 characters?

For far too many, social simply provides one more form of media, one more channel, a new and rich opportunity for distribution. And without respect to the parameters of the channel, it's all part of this thing we call communication. Conceptualize, create, wordsmith, and deliver.

It's worth asking whether our conventional approach to the way we think about connecting (not to mention communicating) with each other actually inhibits the potential of social media. Here's what we mean.

First, we know and embrace the power of words. They can grab attention, connect us, underscore emotion, and even prompt action. Words like mother, father, family, birth, death, and of course, love possess the power to stop us in mid-moment . . . and stir responses we otherwise might scarcely recognize. Given this power, marketers ponder taglines in hopes of the solution that will stir emotion, reach viral proportions, and elicit response. Topical quotations are a favorite connection tactic, because words uttered by someone wiser or more humorous are more potent than words we might string together.

Second, communicators relish the opportunity to articulate and stimulate thought. To that end, we focus on sentence structure, cadence, a strategically positioned pregnant pause, and continuity. Copy is written and rewritten. Speeches are rehearsed, finessed, and re-rehearsed . . . all in pursuit of the message that connects.

Then focus turns to selecting and preparing the idea delivery: the venue, the vehicle, the production, and issues of frequency, market saturation, and multiple channel coverage.

We may not define it this way, but this is how we think about communicating—create and deliver the message to the desired target. Connect and transmit. Or in many cases, connect and convince (or convert).

In fact, marketers both embrace and perpetuate the myth that success can hinge on creative deliverables. It was the genius of the "Just Do It" tagline (with a little credit to the swoosh logo, of course) that turned Nike into a leader in athletic apparel. Never mind the millions invested in market research, target identification, and R&D that gave shape to a multi-year, multi-billion dollar, multi-celebrity anchored marketing campaign.

Apple hit a late-inning home run the moment the company introduced "1000 tunes in your pocket" in the form of the iPod. And much of the success is attributed to award-winning marketing communication.

Companies like Nike and Apple make the formula seem simple: offer a reasonably good product (or service), create a superior message (using a celebrity or two doesn't hurt), and BANG! You've created a winning strategy. We are, after all, talking about marketing.

Where Marketing Goes Awry
Here's the problem: we believe that once we've delivered a message—written it, posted it on a fan page, recorded it, spoken it aloud, hit "send," or organized it into a powerpoint— that we have communicated.

Companies focus on the elevator speech. Sales teams hone the pitch. Public relations experts (not to mention, politicians) pursue the quotable soundbite.

Yet, the foundational principle of communication theory is that connection—the kind that precipitates (or even demands) action—is born in the context of shared experiences. Any marketer can recite the reasons behind the rationale; language, values, fears, and aspirations in large part emanate from experience. They shape the translation and interpretation of the message and are a strong indicator of resulting action.

But in order to identify common language, values, fears, and aspirations, the initial focus of marketing—indeed, any communication enterprise—must be on listening. And far too often, this focus represents a shift—away from predetermined messaging.

What might be the result of an approach to connecting that is intent on listening? How much more rewarding might our communication efforts be if we focused first on the identification of commonalities—of shared experiences?

We call this "intentional listening."

Intentional listening is bigger than focus groups and satisfaction surveys. It's a process rooted in ongoing dialogue, as opposed to monologue. It has as its objective the identification of common ground. It's more about responding than dictating or evangelizing. It's based on the knowledge that listening is the path to the creation of the most effective message.

Marketers intent on listening can find themselves engaged in the kind of conversations around which communities are built, concerns are addressed, and the future envisioned. And for every marketer or organization interested in long-term results, shared aspirations trump fans, followers, and even satisfied customers. That should be incentive enough to begin with listening and encourage ongoing dialogue.

Begin at the Beginning
Any effort to develop an effective social media marketing strategy is built on a listening foundation or platform. As discussed above, one of the great challenges for any marketer is to resist the temptation to bypass the process of laying the foundation and jump straight to the sales proposition.

It's worth noting that the temptation may be especially great for the social media entrepreneur or anyone marketing a product or service born out of personal blood, sweat, and tears. The fact is, the more one believes in what one is selling, the more critical it is to start by listening and to build around a strategy that continues to turn an attentive ear to the marketplace. Why? Because effective listening will define the fabric and dimension of effective messaging.

But this does not come easy. For anyone (or any business) with a point of view, an opinion, a measure of conviction, and the means to disseminate the message, listening is rarely the first or primary step in the marketing and communication process.

From the instant an infant realizes what it takes to relieve the pains of hunger, the practical view of communication focuses on creating and delivering a message. We're conditioned to view charisma, wordsmithing, and creative genius as the stuff of great communication. Listening is what the target audience is supposed to be doing!

The problem is that the success the hungry infant experiences (thanks to the crying message) is not indicative of (or proportionate to) the success of most efforts to market. Parents experience the difficulty inherent in this strategy, as does the ardent evangelist, the door-to-door salesperson, and anyone personally vested in the challenge of conveying a message that calls for action. Effectiveness often seems in direct inverse proportion to how much one talks, how loud the volume, and how intense the need for immediate action.

Effective marketing is a counter-intuitive combination of discipline and art that works exactly opposite of the way we think. It begins when we train our ear on the market with which we desire connection. And whether in a personal or business venue, the discipline of listening is what gives form and function to the creative art of messaging.

This is where it begins. And this is the step to which an effective strategy continually returns. Listen closely, and your target audience will outline what it takes to prompt action.

If communication is the ultimate objective (versus simply being able to lay claim to having broadcast the message), biting your tongue and biding your time will pay dividends— provided you're listening in the interim.

The explosion of social media affords multiple channels that give you a behind-the-scenes ear on the conversations, concerns, aspirations, and experiences of your audience. But this assumes we've identified a target. And if the first temptation is going straight to messaging, a close second is acting as though anyone and everyone we can reach is a viable target. This is almost never the case. Successful marketing almost always includes the proper identification of a key target market. Absent this target identification, listening is rarely effective.

On the other hand, armed with the demographics of a specific target, social media affords the tools that make it possible to listen, learn the language and aspirations of a market, understand the competitive landscape, instigate conversations, and even collaborate with segments of your market in the creation of a message that connects, resonates, and precipitates action.

We should admit that there are, of course, cases when broadcasting (the distribution strategy, not the industry) is appropriate: when making an announcement, when numbers work in your favor, when a brand is strong enough, or a product/service/offering has mass appeal, to acknowledge a few.

But addressing the masses, in spite of its reach, is hardly social media's greatest strength. To view social merely in terms of the message distribution possibilities, however enticing, is to ignore the element that gives it unique standing in the marketplace—its social nature. This is a media that is about conversations, give and take, and most of all, the dynamism that exists in sharing experiences.

A focus on the value of shared experience is certainly not a new idea. Town hall meetings and radio talk shows are practical applications of the fact that communication is not a one-way exercise. Advertisers and marketers have long understood that brand is something much more comprehensive than a tagline, slogan, or great graphic treatment. It speaks to something—often intangible, but nonetheless real—that exists between a company, product or service, and the consumer of same.

Listening for the Social (Shared) Experience

For anyone still wrestling with the role of listening in a social media strategy, this should help bring things into focus. The sharing of experiences is the lifeblood of the inception, growth, and various adaptations of social. Marketers who, caught in the throes of opportunity and possibility, ignore this are doomed to the same levels of success experienced in all other forms of media.

On the other hand, here is one approach to how to identify the experiences your market is most apt to want to share.

1) *Listen to the voice of your target market.* Their messages—the things they care about—may be more important to your marketing strategy than your message.

2) *Stage engagements.* Often the easiest and most effective way to engage your market is by posing a question. What kind of question? See #1 above. Ask questions rooted in the things your market cares about. This accomplishes two things: it provides you with

a growing body of "market intelligence," and it lays the foundation for ongoing shared experiences. If you have trouble coming up with questions that engage your market, you probably need to invest more time on the listening step.

3) *Stage collaboration.* In spite of how this may appear in print, this is "Communication Theory 101." By now, you should be in a position to identify areas where your concerns overlap with those of your market (where your product or service is best positioned to speak to something the market cares about). Invite the market to join in the creation of an answer/solution to an idea/issue that's important to them. If the logistics permit, stage face-to-face collaborative sessions. Where geography, timing, or numbers make this impractical, go online. There are numerous tools and opportunities here—from Twitter chat sessions to LinkedIn group discussions to collaborative sites.

This is a simple, three-step approach; it is by no means the only approach to facilitating shared experiences. The realities of a company, its product or service, and the available resources will have much to do with what the right experience strategy looks like. But the best examples of social media marketing success will increasingly revolve around this strategic building block.

Intentional Listening—the Difference Maker

This book began by noting the first mandate for social media success—to start listening. At the outset of this chapter, we proposed that all listening is not created equal . . . and that zeroing in on the right formula is central to realizing social media's greatest potential.

Consider one more time the differences in the way we listen—to talk radio as you sit in traffic, to a keynote address, to the argument of an adversary, and to the flood of advertising and marketing messages that attempt to connect with us each day.

Listening is done at many levels. But as we become skilled at reactive listening—mixing to a manageable level everything we're taking in—we're inadvertently contributing to the demise of effective communication. As it turns out, it's one of the ingredients we need most if we hope to build relationships that lead to marketing success and long-term customers and clients.

What's missing? Intentional, proactive listening.

Perhaps it's due in part to the fact that we're constantly multitasking. Or perhaps it's a by-product of attempting to pack as much into an hour—even a brief conversation—as possible. Whatever the cause, we rarely think of listening as the centerpiece of business communication, marketing, client development, or sales. Rather, we view marketing as a calculated act of messaging, carefully crafted to convey an idea, iterate services and capabilities, win a decision, or motivate desired actions. Therefore, this is where we invest virtually all the time, budget, and resources that are earmarked for business development and marketing.

As noted throughout this chapter, we are so focused on delivering our message that in those (usually all-too-brief) moments when our target is questioning or commenting—providing insight into what is most important to her—we can't do much better than half listen. Primary attention is being given to the content of our next message—our response.

The poetry and/or profundity of a message has only marginal impact on an audience that is half listening. (Every parent knows this from personal experience.)

If you're wondering how to differentiate your brand, your marketing efforts, and specifically, your social media presence, ask yourself this question: how much more effective might our attempts at communication be if our intent was to find and build around ways to continually listen to the market?

Intentional listening reveals the voice of those with whom we want to connect. And by voice, I mean the cares, aspirations, and concerns of your target audience. It's the key to the most basic principle of effective communication—that connection takes place in the context of shared experience.

Put another way, intentional listening will identify, outline, and define the language of the closest you will ever come to a can't-miss message. And it's the key to the instigation of a whole new brand of experiences—those uniquely shared by you (or your business) and your most coveted customer.

Translation: the shortest distance between where we are today and a relationship that results in the development of stronger brands and better business is less about the construction of a long list of capabilities and more about one or two questions that instigate dialogue. It's less about what we do and more about where our clients live each day. It's less about what we know and more about what we can learn if we'll listen first—and then build experiences that center on ways to continue to listen.

Game-changing social media marketing plans and strategies—not to mention the path to lifetime customers—just might be less about beginning with a compelling marketing message and more about intentional listening.

Eric Fletcher
Eric is the Chief Marketing Officer at McGlinchey Stafford, a national law firm that provides legal counsel and business solutions for companies from coast to coast. His experience spans virtually every aspect of the marketing and communication discipline, from award-winning copy and production in advertising and broadcasting to organizing and successfully leading new business pursuits valued at more than $150,000,000 in the professional service arena. Eric has provided strategic planning and consulting to local entrepreneurs and Fortune 100 companies, B2B and B2C enterprises, and two of the world's largest professional service organizations. As a law firm CMO, Eric employs this experience with two primary objectives: to expand proactive business development strategies in a way that stimulates organic growth and to protect and enhance the brand of the firm. Over the past two decades, Eric's track record includes successful major target pursuits, the direction of large client team efforts for international consulting organizations, and for the past dozen years, Am Law 100 and NLJ 250 law firms. Eric is recognized as one of the Top 100 CMOs on Twitter. He authors the popular blog, Marketing Brain Fodder.

Afterword

By Liz K. Miller

Do you remember your first time with social media?

For me, it was in 1993 when I first logged into an AOL chat room that had formed around indoor soccer. At that time, I had just started working for the now-defunct Continental Indoor Soccer League (CISL), where our online goal was clear—get anyone talking about soccer if you could. And lots of people were talking in these rooms.

Conversations ranged from last night's game to which team would reach the championship. But then came the day when I panicked because there was an *intensely* negative conversation starting about the CISL, launching me into crisis mode.

So, in a rash move, I created a fake identity and started a war of words. Within just a few days, my fake identity was revealed, and I was labeled as a fraud, "self-serving," and "underhanded" and was actually asked to "leave" the room and not return. "This room was for fans—not for frauds."

I got a heartfelt e-mail from one of the regulars in the chat saying that 1) I shouldn't have pretended to be someone I wasn't, 2) I should have left the negative comments to the fans—they would have handled it soon enough, and 3) I would have been welcomed into the conversation if I had just been honest.

In the end, I learned to listen, build trust, form relationships, deliver value, and listen again. Sound familiar? While the eight mandates that Kent Huffman outlines in the pages of this book are fundamental to social media success, I would argue that they are fundamental to broader marketing success. I would also argue that marketers must focus more on the fundamental strategy than the technology or even fast-moving customer expectations.

According to research conducted by the Chief Marketing Officer (CMO) Council*, fewer than 17% of marketers surveyed believed their social media strategy was fully integrated and meshed with overall marketing strategy. Like the "me of 1993," 27% of marketers are concerned that they can't control what's being said about their brand or how their brand is being used in this wild, customer-driven world. In fact, 29% of marketers believe that customers engage via social media to complain about a bad experience. In the end, there is still that fear that the negative impact will wash away any of the positive word of mouth that social might bring about.

When consumers were asked why they engaged, only 8% said it was to complain. But a staggering 80% say they want to engage so they can actually try new things based on their friends' suggestions. And 74% want to engage to share their positive experiences and make a difference for the brands they love, which should be enough to wash away some of those fears.

So, if I could write an e-mail to "1993 Liz," here's what I'd want to say:

Dear Liz,

Listening is both the first and last of eight mandates for marketing success. It is the single most important key for those who want to be successful in social media. Too many marketers jump right in and start using various social media tools before they've even developed a plan. Don't make that mistake!

Remember, a true relationship has to be earned. It's about respect and trust. And success relies largely on the bond of trust generated between customer and company.

Leaders are most often valued and respected for their knowledge, experience, passion, and vision. So you have to put the "right stuff" out there to attract and grow an audience. Building a loyalty community of fans and followers is not a snap-your-finger deal.

Generating reliable performance metrics will become a major priority. "What's the ROI from all that social media stuff you are doing?" your boss will ask. You may not know today, but in tomorrow's hyper-competitive environment and generally weak economy, generating measurable, repeatable value will no longer be an option for marketers.

So remember one thing—all listening is not created equal.

Yours truly,
Future Liz

P.S. You don't win the mega-million lottery in 2012. Sorry.

If you don't recognize the messages I would deliver to myself, immediately return to page 19 and start reading again, because you've missed the real keys to success that this book outlines. In fact, my letter is wholly plagiarized from the starting paragraphs of each of this book's chapters, because the advice is sound, and the message is exactly on point. These eight mandates and the supporting insights, advice, and success stories that have been collected from 155 (including Kent) of the world's most innovative—and inspirational—marketers reach well beyond social media and drop us head first into the eight mandates critical for ANY marketing success.

My hope is that reaching the conclusion of this book marks your renewed commitment to continuing this journey through the land of social, like it has for me. Just remember—you're not alone in the struggles you face. And most importantly, there really is a pot of gold at the end of the rainbow for those who listened, learned, and repeated.

Liz K. Miller

Liz Miller oversees the daily operations, programs, research, and strategy of the Chief Marketing Officer (CMO) Council and its special interest networks. Liz's career spans more than 19 years in the sports, entertainment, retail, health, beauty, and personal care industries. She has worked with brands, sponsors, and clients like Pepsi, KFC, Darden Brands, Snickers, Playboy Enterprises, El Pollo Loco, Nike, Budweiser, the City of San Jose, BioForm Medical, Jan Marini Skin Research, Forum Boxing, White Cap Direct, IBM, Accenture, Xerox, Catalina Marketing, Deloitte, Oracle, HP, and more to develop thought leadership, branding, and communications to reach a broad range of customers on an international scale. When Liz isn't writing, tweeting, tweaking, or freaking out about marketing, she's corralling her two large Akitas and enjoying life in her native California.

Data is from the report "The Variance in the Social Brand Experience." 2011. CMO Council.

Acknowledgements

In addition to all the marketing pros who contributed their insights and success stories throughout this book, I also owe a huge debt of gratitude to a number of other generous people who helped, inspired, and encouraged me along the way. Thank you, my friends!

Dr. David Aaker
Dr. Jennifer Aaker
Andrés Silva Arancibia
Alicia Arenas
Michael Brenner
Dr. Laura Bright
Cheryl Burgess
Lida Citroën
Sima Dahl
John Dragoon
John Ellett
Bear Files
Selma Filipović
Dr. Raymond Fisk
Eric Fletcher
John Foley, Jr.
Hope Frank
Lois Geller
Ian Gertler

Glen Gilmore
Dr. Dean Anthony Gratton
Dr. Sarah-Jayne Gratton
Jeffrey Hayzlett
Chris Herbert
Amy Howell
Judy Huffman
Linda Ireland
Mike Johansson
Dave Kerpen
Ed Lallo
Beto Lima
Kathy Magrino
Chuck Martin
Liz Miller
Margaret Molloy
Erin Mulligan Nelson
Gail Nelson
Bill Newton

Eve Mayer Orsburn
Berenice Ring
Tony Roberts
Dr. Jessica Rogers
Alex Romanovich
Ted Rubin
Renay San Miguel
Mark Schaefer
Dr. Gary Schirr
Alan See
Andy Smith
Frank Strong
Patrick Strother
Hollis Thomases
Teri Lucie Thompson
Coylene Turlington
Dr. William Ward
Deborah Weinstein
Patricia Wilson

1531284R00069

Made in the USA
San Bernardino, CA
27 December 2012